YARN CRAFTS

YARN CRAFTS

Easy Instructions for 30 Bright & Beautiful DIY Projects

INCLUDING WREATHS, TASSELS, RAINBOWS, POM-POM GARLANDS & MORE

SARAH FREEMAN

BETTER DAY BOOKS®
HAPPY • CREATIVE • CURATED

Publisher: Peg Couch
Cover Designer: Lindsay Hess
Book Designer: Llara Pazdan
Editor: Colleen Dorsey

Library of Congress Control Number: 2025939990

ISBN: 978-0-7643-7065-6
Printed in India
10 9 8 7 6 5 4 3 2 1

Published by Better Day Books, an imprint of Schiffer Publishing, Ltd.

Better Day Books
Email: hello@betterdaybooks.com
Web: www.betterdaybooks.com
Visit us on Instagram!
@better_day_books

Schiffer Publishing
4880 Lower Valley Road
Atglen, PA 19310
Phone: 610-593-1777
Fax: 610-593-2002
Email: info@schifferbooks.com
Web: www.schifferbooks.com

For our complete selection of fine books on this and related subjects, please visit our website at www.betterdaybooks.com. You may also write for a free catalog.

Better Day Books titles are available at special discounts for bulk purchases for sales promotions or premiums. Special editions, including personalized covers, corporate imprints, and excerpts, can be created in large quantities for special needs. For more information, contact the publisher.

Dedication

To my kids, for being my best craft buddies and endless inspiration. To my mom, who taught me to love yarn and all things handmade. And to Josh, for always cheering me on and believing in all my crafty dreams.

CONTENTS

28

YAY
36

40

56

76

102

112

thankful
126

144

WELCOME

Hey there! Welcome to *Handmade Happiness Yarn Crafts*! This book is special to me not only because I love yarn and crafting, but also because it is my first book! The process of writing this book has been a new, exciting adventure for me, and I'm thrilled to share about one of my passions.

I have loved crafting since I was a young girl, and I have dabbled in many different types of arts and crafts. I had a whole cupboard of craft supplies in my bedroom, and coming up with new projects was one of my favorite activities. My parents were also very creative, and my mom would take me with her to yarn shops and craft stores. She particularly loved crochet and knitting, and there was always plenty of yarn in our house.

I didn't fall in love with yarn until I was pregnant with my fourth child. It was then that I began crocheting; I found that it was the perfect way to relax and decompress at the end of the day. Yarn is so cozy and soft, and that just added to the comfort. After making a few blankets, I had quite a bit of leftover yarn. I made a few pom-pom garlands with the leftover yarn and was amazed when I was able to sell them in my Etsy shop. I ended up making and selling many more pom-pom garlands over the next few years, and my love of yarn was officially sparked.

My business has now evolved toward helping others find joy in creating. Many of the projects on my website involve yarn, since I love coming up with new ways to use it. I wanted to write this book for those who want to use yarn in their crafting but who don't necessarily want to crochet or knit. I love crochet, but sometimes I enjoy a project that doesn't take as long as a crocheted blanket. I wanted to make these projects accessible and easy for all ages and levels of crafting experience. In this book, we will explore some of the many ways yarn can be used, including making pom-poms and tassels, weaving, cross-stitching, faux embroidery, creating art pieces, crafting home décor, and many more!

I believe in the power of craft therapy, and I hope that these projects help you feel the joy, calm, and confidence that come with creating. As with all crafts, the projects in this book can be personalized to fit your style and tastes. Use colors and textures that bring you joy and make each project your own. This book can even be a starting point for designing your own yarn projects!

Thank you again for picking up this book! I hope you enjoy creating these projects, and I hope it sparks even more creativity. Here's to some colorful, cozy crafting!

Love,

MEET THE AUTHOR

We sat down with Sarah to learn a little more about her and her journey. Join us!

What's your story? What led you to this art form?

I have always loved crafting. When I was young, I would have happily spent all my babysitting money at art and craft stores. In the thick of motherhood with three little girls under the age of seven, I learned how to crochet. It was a calming and therapeutic practice for me, and I got hooked (no pun intended!). Crochet led to pom-poms, which led to my Etsy shop and selling pom-pom garlands. My business was built primarily on pom-pom garlands for the first few years, then it evolved into creating crafting tutorials. While I'm no longer selling pom-poms, my love of yarn has only increased, and I am always drawn to crafts that use yarn.

Your designs are so cheerful and fun. What inspires them?

As I've gotten older, I've embraced the fact that I love color. There were years when I wrongly thought that wearing bright colors or decorating with bright colors wasn't very mature. Bright, vibrant colors give me joy, and life is too short not to enjoy the colors I love! I am always inspired by the colors around me: in flowers, in pieces of art, in a pattern on a quilt or rug, or even in the produce section of the grocery store. I love pairing colors together to see what unexpected pairings work well. Finding the right color palette is almost the hardest part for me when creating projects, because I love them all and want to use all the colors!

What is your workspace like?

I have a very happy craft room where I do most of my creating. I have an entire bookcase filled with yarn (stacked in rainbow order), and I truly love the joy it brings to the room. I also have shelves with bins of beads, sequins, trims, and paints; spools of ribbon hanging on another wall; and a cartful of overflow yarn. While I have two desks in the room, I actually do most of my crafting on the floor, since my yarn doesn't roll around as much. I almost always have an audiobook going while I'm creating, and I love to have a drink handy (Diet Dr. Pepper is my fave). My craft room inspires me and motivates me to get work done. My kids also use the space for their crafts, and even though I'm often cleaning up their craft messes, I love that they find joy in creating too.

What appeals to you most about yarn as a medium? Do you have any yarn (or crafting) tips that might surprise us?

Yarn is so versatile. I think that most people see yarn only as a supply for crochet or knitting, but there are so many other uses! I love that its fluid structure makes it easy to twist, tie, stitch, and glue into many different creations. It is a relatively inexpensive medium, since one skein of yarn can go a long way. I also love how yarn can be found in hundreds of colors and textures. Two tips that I would suggest with yarn are to have a good pair of scissors and to embrace using hot glue. If your scissors aren't sharp enough, it will be harder to trim a pom-pom or cut a clean yarn end, and your projects will take longer. Similarly, hot glue is an amazing tool for yarn. Yarn adheres well with hot glue, and it helps speed up the process.

What is one piece of advice you wish you had heard early on in your maker journey?

Think outside the box! I love a crafting challenge, and some of my favorite projects came from trying to create something unexpected. During the early days of my pom-pom-making business, I bought a cute, ceramic berry basket. I thought it would be so adorable to fill the basket with pom-pom strawberries. Through trial and error, I finally made a pom-pom strawberry that ended up being a bestseller in my shop. From that idea, other pom-poms were born: watermelons, cherries, pineapples, and cacti. If there is something you love, think of ways you can make that item using unexpected supplies or tools. The results can be really rewarding!

What do you hope readers will take away from this book?

I hope that this book will open readers' eyes to the joy of creating. There is something therapeutic in taking time to make something, and I hope this book helps readers find joy and fulfillment in working on and completing a project. I also hope that these projects spark creativity and can help inspire more making. Whether it's encouraging more yarn crafts or expanding projects into other mediums, I want this book to be a starting point for more crafting!

1

GETTING STARTED

In this section of the book, you'll learn all the basics you need to know about yarn, meet the tools and supplies that will help you craft beautiful projects with yarn, and learn how to make pom-poms and tassels step by step. You'll be set up for success and ready to craft!

YARN 101

Since yarn is at the heart of everything we do in this book, we need to put it first and talk about how amazing it is! Not only can it be found online or in any craft store, but it also comes in so many unique thicknesses, textures, and colors. For many projects, only a fraction of a skein is used up, so one skein can be used to make numerous projects. Once you start working with yarn, you'll develop a taste for certain types that you enjoy the most. Each of the projects in this book provides an estimate of how much yarn you'll need to complete it. These amounts may vary, though, depending on the type of yarn used and the size of your individual project. And, because each yarn varies in weight, stretch, and texture, remember that the amounts suggested throughout are only approximations. As a rule of thumb, it is better to have too much yarn on hand than too little! Yarn can easily be cut, but it is harder to piece it together.

A • OMEGACRYL: Omegacryl is composed of three separate, very thin strings. It is delicate and can break if all three strands are not used together. It comes in vibrant colors that are often hard to find in regular yarn, and it makes great tassels, pom-poms, and small-scale projects. It's easiest to buy this online, since it is not often stocked in stores.

B • EYELASH OR TINSEL YARN: Eyelash yarn gets its name from the thin fringe that is attached to a thicker string. While a bit messy to work with, eyelash yarn is perfect for any scrappy yarn projects, since it resembles tinsel or feathers. For pops of silver or gold in your projects, look for eyelash yarn with metallic fringe.

C • ACRYLIC MEDIUM-WEIGHT YARN: This is the most versatile yarn that can be used in almost every project in this book! Acrylic yarn makes great pom-poms and tassels, glues well, and comes in almost

every color of the rainbow. It is also commonly used in crochet and knitting.

D • COTTON YARN: Cotton yarn usually comes in a medium weight. While similar in weight to medium-weight acrylic yarn, it doesn't fluff up quite as well. It is primarily used in crochet and knitting and washes well. If you're using cotton yarn for pom-poms, combine it with an acrylic yarn to help fluff it up.

E • HOMESPUN MEDIUM-WEIGHT YARN: Homespun yarn has a wavy texture and is very soft. It is best used in projects where the wavy texture can be seen, like in tassels or glued-yarn projects. This variety also looks great in scrappy projects where other yarn is also used.

F • MEDIUM-WEIGHT ROVING: This yarn is often made from wool or acrylic. Roving is great for adding texture or mixing with other varieties of yarn. Since it is not twisted as tightly as regular yarn, it can be pulled apart more easily and can feel rough. When using it, be careful not to pull too hard, since it can become separated if pulled too firmly.

G • BULKY-WEIGHT ACRYLIC YARN: This yarn is softer than medium-weight acrylic yarn and almost as versatile. Bulky acrylic can be used for almost every project in this book and has a beautiful texture. The bulkiness of this yarn lends itself well to cozy projects.

H • T-SHIRT YARN: Made from the same material as a T-shirt, this stretchy yarn doesn't really behave like most yarn—it is more like elastic than yarn. Still, it can be used for gift wrapping or large-scale projects. It also looks cute in yarn flags or scrappy pom-poms.

I • CHENILLE OR POLYESTER BULKY YARN: This yarn is great for larger-scale projects. It is one individual strand, so it doesn't fray at the end like other yarn. It's very soft to the touch, responds well to hot glue, and is great for faux-embroidery projects.

J • ROVING-STYLE BULKY YARN: Bulky roving yarn can be made from wool or acrylic. It's more flexible than knit bulky yarn, but it can break if pulled too hard. It creates a more fluffy-looking project and is great for large-scale projects.

K • FINGER-LOOP YARN: Usually made from polyester, this yarn has loops that can be used for finger weaving. It is great for adding variety to hanging-yarn projects and also makes great wreaths. Online is the best place to shop for this yarn, since it is harder to find in stores.

L • KNIT SUPER-BULKY YARN: Many strands are woven into one for this yarn, so the ends have a tendency to unravel. It's great for large-scale projects, especially ones with glue, since the glue keeps the ends from fraying.

HELPFUL TOOLS AND SUPPLIES

When working with yarn, certain tools and materials just make the process easier. Many of these tools will show up again and again in this book's projects. These are, of course, only suggestions, though. For example, if you prefer to use one glue over another, do it! Find the tools that work best for you.

A • PLASTIC POM-POM MAKERS: Pom-pom makers are probably one of my most used craft tools. Available in many different sizes, plastic makers help you create pom-poms easily. Any brand works well, but Clover is my favorite.

B • CARDBOARD POM-POM MAKERS: When making larger pom-poms, or if you don't want to purchase plastic makers, cardboard makers are great. Cardboard makers require a little more careful crafting, since the cardboard doesn't hold the cut yarn in place while tying, but they still get the job done.

C • WOODEN OR PLASTIC TASSEL MAKER: Tassel makers come in a variety of materials. Store-bought makers are nice because they can easily make tassels of the same length. Often, tassel makers can be used for making pom-poms as well. Yarn can be tied in the center of the wound yarn, then pulled off and trimmed into a pom-pom.

D • CARDBOARD TASSEL MAKER: Even though a piece of cardboard isn't very fancy, it does the trick for making a perfect tassel. Cardboard can be cut into any length, which helps with keeping tassels uniform in length.

E • SCISSORS: A great pair of scissors is a must for any crafter. Heavy-duty, sharp scissors are needed for every project in this book. These are used for trimming pom-poms and tassels in addition to cutting all yarn.

F • EMBROIDERY SCISSORS: Sharp, pointy scissors are a necessity for making pom-poms. These are used for cutting the yarn off the maker, since thin scissors are needed to get in the gap between the two halves of the maker.

G • RULER OR MEASURING TAPE: For some projects, specific lengths of yarn are needed, and a ruler or measuring tape is convenient for measuring accurately. While I often like to just approximate, it is nice to have a ruler handy for certain projects.

H • HOT-GLUE GUN AND GLUE STICKS: A hot-glue gun is probably my second-most-used craft supply. The projects in this book use a lot of hot glue. Yarn sticks well with hot glue, and it is a much-quicker way to attach yarn than with school glue or stitching. Make sure to take care when using hot glue around children.

I • SCHOOL GLUE: While hot glue is an easy and fast way to secure yarn, school glue has a place in many of the projects in this book. For small details, school glue is often better than hot glue, since it is easier to apply to small surfaces and the items can be rearranged before it dries.

J • CLEAR TAPE: Tape is a supply that is probably already in your craft drawer or office. Clear tape is used in several of the projects in this book, since it holds yarn well and can't be seen easily.

K • WASHI TAPE: I love having washi tape on hand for different projects. The thing that sets it apart from clear tape is that it can be easily removed. Some of the projects in this book require tape to hold items in place temporarily.

L • METAL YARN NEEDLE: A metal yarn needle with a large eye is very useful when working with yarn. Because a metal needle is sharper than a plastic needle, it is great for stringing yarn through pom-poms or tassels.

M • PLASTIC YARN NEEDLE: For the projects that don't require a sharp yarn needle, a plastic one is a great tool. These also have a large eye, which makes threading yarn easy yarn. Plastic needles are also better than metal ones for crafting with children.

G
A
C
D
I
ELMER'S
WASHABLE, NO RUN
SCHOOL GLUE
Safe | Nontoxic
4 fl oz (118 mL)
B
H
TILSWALL
M
L
F
J
K
E

HOW TO MAKE A TASSEL

materials

- **Yarn**: about 8 yards (7.3 m) of medium-weight acrylic yarn to make one 4" (10 cm) tassel (amount will vary depending on the weight of the yarn and the length and thickness of the tassel)
- **Tassel maker or a piece of cardboard cut to the desired tassel length**
- **Scissors**

Tassels are one of the easiest yarn techniques to master. Because tassels can be made in so many lengths and widths, they are easily adapted for many projects, from bag charms and gift toppers to spooky ghosts and Christmas ornaments. While tassel makers made out of wood or plastic can be purchased in stores or online, a piece of cardboard you have on hand works just as well. Cardboard can even be used to make tassels of varying lengths, whereas a wooden maker makes just one tassel size. For the largest tassels, even your arm or two chair legs can be used for wrapping!

Wooden Tassel Maker

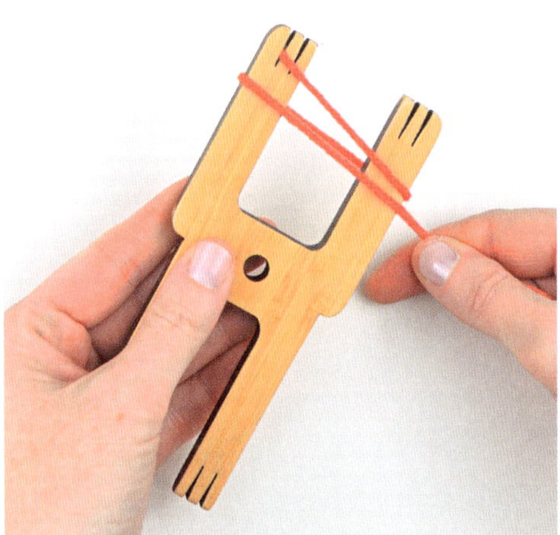

1 **Wrap the yarn around the prongs of the tassel maker.** Hold on to one end of the tassel maker while wrapping yarn around the prongs until the yarn is secure on the maker. The thicker the yarn and the more yarn you use, the thicker the tassel will be.

2 **Tie the yarn together.** Cut a separate, short piece of yarn. Insert it into the center of the yarn loops and tie a knot on top of one side of the yarn loops. If you're using thick yarn, use a thinner piece of yarn or string for tying. Then remove the yarn from the maker.

3 **Tie yarn around the tassel.** Using another separate piece of yarn, tie a knot around all the loops about ½" (1.5 cm) down from the top. This creates a little "bobble" at the top and cinches the tassel together.

4 **Cut through the loops.** With scissors, cut through all the loops at the bottom of the tassel. Try to pull the loops as taut as possible with the scissors before cutting them so that the ends turn out as even in length as possible.

5 **Even out the ends.** Trim the ends to make the tassel even at the bottom. This is like giving the tassel a haircut. Hold all the ends with one hand and, with the scissors in the other hand, cut across. The tassel is now complete!

Cardboard Tassel Maker

1 **Wrap the yarn around the piece of cardboard.** Like when using a tassel maker, wrap yarn around the length of the cardboard. Cardboard can be cut to any size to make shorter or longer tassels. When you're done wrapping, slide the yarn off the cardboard, being careful to keep the circular shape.

2 **Tie a knot at the top of the tassel.** Cut a separate, short piece of yarn. Insert it into the center of the yarn loops, making sure not to miss any, and tie a knot on top of one side of the yarn loops. This will be the top of the tassel. To complete the tassel, follow steps 3–5 for the wooden tassel maker.

HOW TO MAKE A POM-POM

materials

- **Yarn:** amount will vary depending on the size of the maker and the weight of the yarn, but on average with medium-weight acrylic yarn:
  - For a 1" (2.5 cm) pom-pom: 8 yards (7.3 m)
  - For a 2" (5 cm) pom-pom: 18 yards (16.5 m)
  - For a 3 ½" (9 cm) pom-pom: 42 yards (38.4 m)
- **Plastic pom-pom maker or cardboard pom-pom maker**
- **Embroidery scissors or other pointy, sharp scissors for cutting pom-pom off maker**
- **Trimming scissors**

Pom-poms are where it all started for me! My whole business was sparked by creating some yarn pom-poms out of scrap yarn. Little did I know where those pom-poms would take me! I am obviously a big fan of the pom-pom, and I use them anywhere and everywhere. I string them on garlands, make giant ones for ornaments, use them as embellishments . . . the possibilities are endless! Like a tassel, a pom-pom can be made with a plastic pom-pom maker or with a handmade cardboard maker. Once you learn how to make a pom-pom, you can experiment with different sizes and different types of yarn.

Plastic Pom-Pom Maker

1 Wrap one side of the pom-pom maker. Open only one-half of the pom-pom maker and begin wrapping yarn around the semicircle. Hold on to the loose end of the yarn until it gets covered so that it stays put.

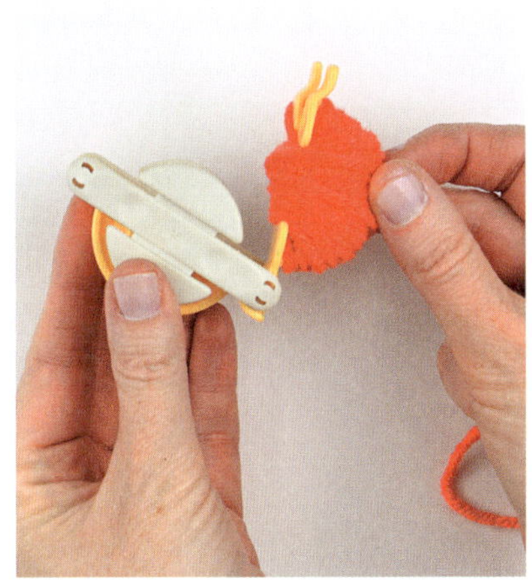

2 **Fill the whole half with yarn.** Continue wrapping until the half is full. For fuller pom-poms, fill a little fuller, but make sure the maker will still close. The arc in the center of the half should be completely filled in. Close the half and cut the yarn.

3 **Wrap the other half.** Wind yarn around the second half just as you did the first. Fill the entire side so that it is similar in size to the other half. Close the maker and cut the yarn.

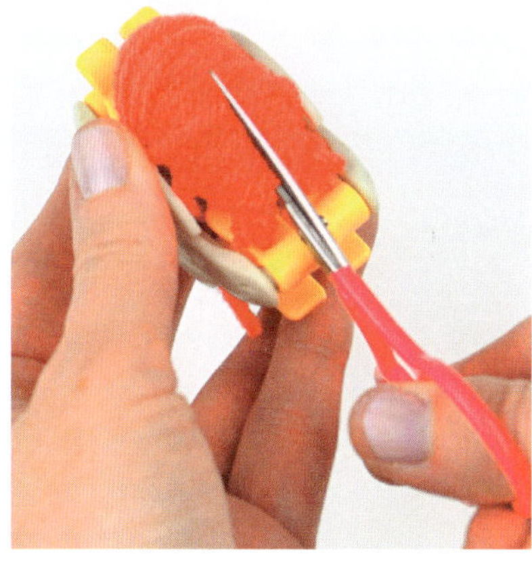

4 **Cut the pom-pom off the maker.** With embroidery scissors, begin cutting through the layers of yarn on one-half, using the groove in the maker as a guide. Be careful to hold on to the maker so that it doesn't accidentally open. Repeat with the other half.

5 **Tie the pom-pom together.** Feed a new piece of yarn through the grooves in the center of the pom-pom maker. Pull the yarn very tightly and double-knot it—If this yarn is too loose, the pom-pom could fall apart! Make sure the knot is as tight as possible.

6 **Trim.** Remove the pom-pom from the maker by opening both halves and pulling apart. Use your second pair of sharp scissors to trim around the pom-pom and shorten any long ends.

7 **Finish the pom-pom.** Continue trimming and fluff as you go to make sure no long hidden ends get missed.

Cardboard Pom-Pom Maker

1 Cut two "C" shapes out of cardboard. Cut two fat "C" shapes as shown. Sturdier cardboard works best for this—flimsy cardboard, like that from a cereal box, may bend too easily. Make sure each "C" is similar in size. Stack them onto each other before you start wrapping.

2 Wrap the yarn around the cardboard. Holding the end, wrap yarn through the center of the "C" and around the outside. The maker is full when the center of the maker is totally filled. Don't worry about covering all the cardboard, since it will fill in when the pom-pom is cut.

3 Cut through the yarn. Holding the yarn tightly with one hand, use embroidery or pointy scissors to cut the yarn in the groove between the two pieces of cardboard. Don't let go of the yarn—it will try to come undone once it has been cut.

4 Tie the pom-pom. While still holding the pom-pom maker in one hand, carefully insert a new piece of yarn in between the two pieces of cardboard and pull tightly around all the yarn. You can let go of the maker at this point. Tie a tight double knot.

5 Remove the pom-pom from the maker. Use the opening of the "C" shape to remove the cardboard from the pom-pom. To complete the pom-pom, follow steps 6–7 for the plastic pom-pom maker.

LOOME

2

PROJECTS

In this section of the book, you'll find dozens of projects to make, customize, enjoy, and share. Each project includes a full materials list, including recommended yarn types, and clear step-by-step instructions. Feel free to jump around from project to project and to adapt designs to your own preferences!

materials + tools

- Yarn
  - Various textures and weights
  - Various colors
  - Scraps and bits work great!
- **Canvas or cardboard**
- **Paint**
- **Paintbrush**
- **Hot-glue gun**
- **School glue**
- **Scissors**
- **Pom-poms, trims, or other embellishments (optional)**

ABSTRACT YARN ART

We have a lot of art lovers in my family, so when we take family vacations, we like to seek out the local art museums and spend a few hours browsing. To be honest, some of my kids enjoy this more than others! We took a family trip to New York a few years ago and visited the MOMA, where we enjoyed the modern abstract art. I particularly enjoyed mixed-media pieces that incorporated yarn or other textiles. For this project, we are using yarn to make our own abstract art. Thanks to the bright colors, the flexibility, and the many textures of yarn, it lends itself perfectly to abstract art. The designs in my piece are simply suggestions. Create your own patterns and designs by using colors that fit your personality and décor. This project is a great one to do with kids as well.

1 Paint the canvas. Paint the canvas with a color of your choosing, or just leave it white if desired. Multiple colors could even be used for a more detailed piece, but a single solid color will allow a variety of yarns to shine.

2 Hot-glue larger yarn pieces to the canvas. Start with your largest yarn pieces first. To make half pom-poms like the one shown, use just one-half of a pom-pom maker and complete like normal. Hot glue works best for larger yarn pieces.

3 Create spirals. Using hot glue again, spiral some yarn and glue it into place. If the yarn is thin, school glue can work, but for thicker yarn, hot glue is best. Make the spirals large or small to fit the space.

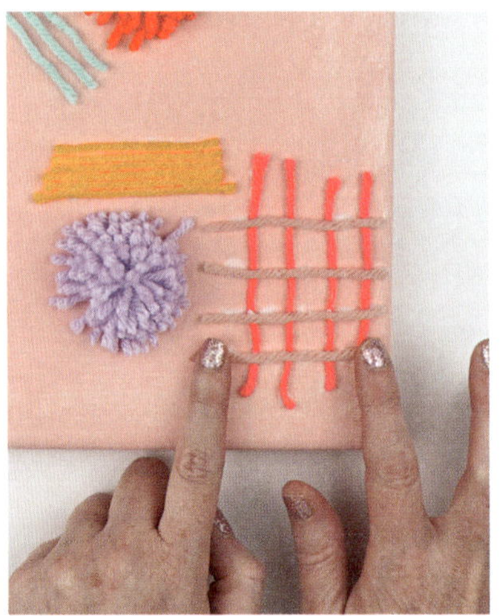

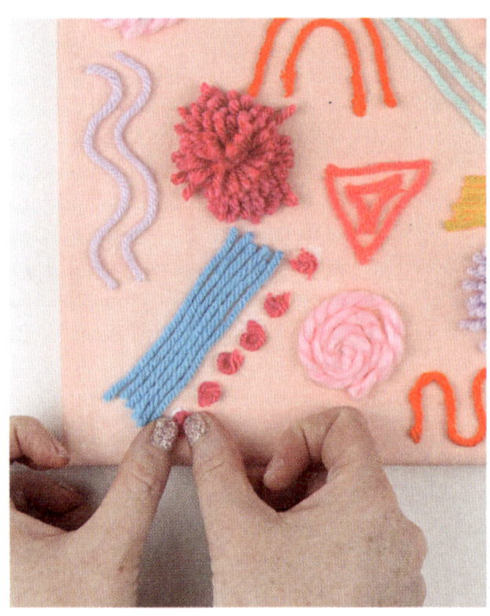

4 Glue lines of yarn. Create designs with straight lines. The lines can be bunched together or separated. Make shapes out of the lines like the arrow design shown here. School glue works well for light-to-medium-weight yarn.

5 Make a grid. By layering lines of yarn, you can create grid patterns. Use one single color for a grid or different colors for more variety. Grids can fill a lot of space because they can be made to fit any size.

6 Add more shapes. Make wavy designs, rainbow-like arcs, and circles with yarn. Small spaces can also be filled with little bits of yarn twisted into circles. Remember to vary the texture and size of your yarn for more visual appeal.

7 **Fill in empty spaces.** Look over your piece and fill in any spots that feel sparse or unbalanced. This piece can be as busy or as simple as you'd like. Make sure that all the yarn is secure, and add extra glue to the ends to keep them from fraying.

tip

Use up scraps of yarn for this project!

GREETINGS FROM
CALIFORNIA!
21

PLASTIC CANVAS RAINBOWS

materials + tools

- **Yarn**
  - Medium-weight acrylic or cotton
  - 6 colors
  - For a 9" (23 cm) diameter rainbow: about 60–65 yards (54.9–59.4 m)
- **Plastic canvas circle in any size**
- **Scissors**
- **Metal yarn needle with large eye**
- **Pom-pom trim, pom-poms, and ribbon for embellishments (optional)**
- **Hot-glue gun (optional)**

When I was about ten years old, I learned how to cross-stitch. To help me learn the stitches, my mom bought me a piece of plastic canvas and some yarn. Plastic canvas has larger spaces for working the stitches, isn't flimsy like cloth, and provides an easy way to learn the technique. I remember my mom also buying me a book of plastic-canvas crafts, which featured things like tissue-box covers and door hangers. When I came across a circular plastic canvas at a craft store a few years ago, those memories came rushing back. I knew that I wanted to make something with that canvas, and I knew that a rainbow would be perfect! While this project uses backstitch rather than cross-stitch, it is just as easy to pick up. Once you master the technique, use your favorite color combinations to make your rainbow unique!

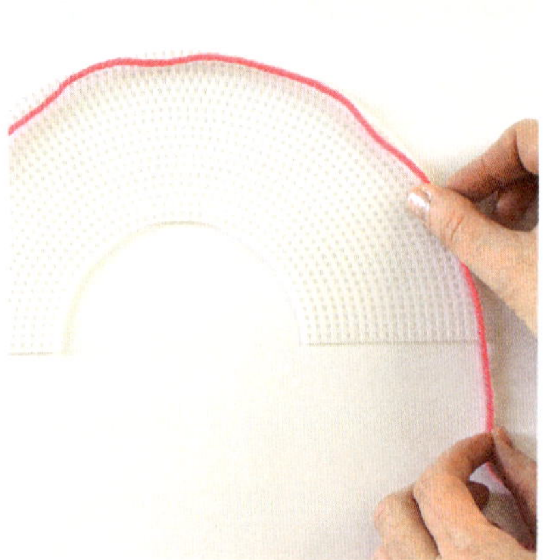

1 Cut the plastic circle in half. Find the centerline and cut carefully along it. Each circle can make two rainbows: one half will have the little vertical lines of plastic at the bottom, but don't worry about cutting them off—the yarn will cover those small pieces.

2 Cut an arc out of the center. The rainbow can also be kept as a solid half circle, but, if desired, cut an arc out of the center. If you want to end up with even sections of each yarn color, count the rows to make sure the small arc leaves an even number.

3 Measure the yarn. Lay the yarn around the edge of the canvas with about 6" (15 cm) extra at the bottom on each side. Multiply that length by four to get your approximate amount for each row. The yarn will be doubled up on the needle.

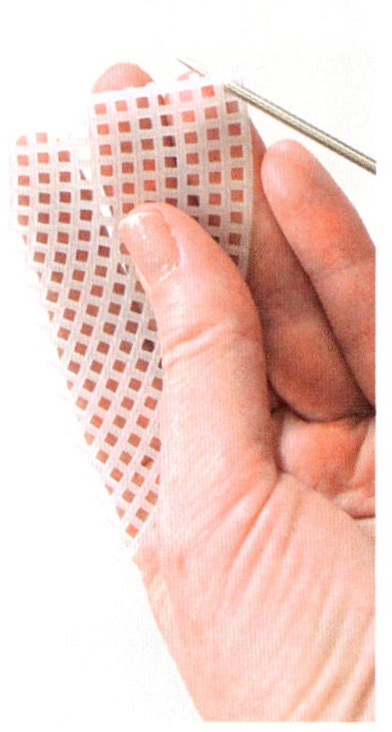

4 Insert the needle into the first square. Doubling up the yarn on the needle and without tying any knots, insert the needle into the first square on the front side of the canvas. Pull the yarn through, leaving a few inches of fringe at the bottom.

5 Begin backstitching. Skipping one to three squares, insert the needle from the backside of the canvas and pull the yarn through, holding the fringe as you do so to ensure you don't accidentally pull it out.

6 Complete the stitch. To complete the first backstitch, insert the needle back into the first square on the front, where the fringe is and where you started. The first stitch is now complete!

7 Repeat steps 5–6 all the way around. Skip one to three squares and insert the needle from the backside. Pull through and insert from the front into the square where the previous stitch ends. Continue this way to the end of the row.

8 Finish the row. To make sure the fringe all comes out of the front of the canvas, always end each row by pulling the needle and yarn through the back to the front in the last square. Now repeat steps 3–8 for all rows of the same color!

9 Repeat steps 3–8 in new colors. For all subsequent colors, backstitch all around the rainbow using the same technique. Make sure that the first and last square always have the fringe coming out of the front of the rainbow.

10 Trim the ends. To even out the fringe, cut across it with sharp scissors. You can set a large ruler or a book on top of the rainbow to help you get an even cut—the extra weight and straight edge will make the trimming easier.

11 Add embellishments. If desired, hot-glue pom-pom trim, ribbon, or whatever embellishments you like to the back of the rainbow. Pom-poms can be hot-glued to the front. Other options include sequins, bows, ribbon, tassels, buttons, or beads.

YAY

WANDS AND PENNANTS

I have recently been loving the pennant flags that I keep seeing pop up in boutiques and souvenir shops. The flags are usually made from felt and have names of places or simple graphics on them. While these pennants are darling on their own, I knew they could be made even better with a pom-pom added! This same technique can be used to make pom-pom wands by simply removing the flag. I love that this project is great for a party or large group, since everyone can customize their own. To make it simpler for children, pom-poms could be made ahead of time, and adults can help with the hot glue. Kids can choose their own pom-poms, glitter colors, and embellishments. These pennants and wands are perfect for dress-up, party décor or favors, or bedroom décor.

materials + tools

- Yarn
  - Light, medium, or bulky weight; multiple weights can be combined into one pom-pom
  - 1–5 colors per pom-pom
  - For a 3 ½" (9 cm) pom-pom: about 42 yards (38.4 m) of medium acrylic yarn*
- Felt (firmer felt works well)
- Pencil or marker
- Scissors
- Wooden dowels
- Hot-glue gun
- 3 ½" (9 cm) pom-pom maker
- Embroidery scissors
- Scrap yarn and ribbons
- School glue
- Glitter
- Flag template on page 162

*Yarn amounts will vary depending on the weight of yarn and size of pom-pom maker.

Pennant

1 Cut out the flag. Using the template on page 162, trace the flag shape onto a piece of felt. Cut the shape out with sharp scissors. You could also choose to enlarge the flag if you have firmer felt, but if the felt is too floppy, a larger flag will droop.

2 Glue the flag to the dowel. Add a line of hot glue about ½" (1.5 cm) in from the edge of the flag. Glue the dowel to the felt, leaving 1" (2.5 cm) of dowel sticking out at the top. This is where the pom-pom will be attached.

3 Wrap the felt around the dowel. Apply a little more hot glue between the dowel and the edge of the felt, then wrap this edge around the dowel. If you're using very firm felt, hold the felt in place until the hot glue has completely hardened.

4 Apply hot glue to the pom-pom. Make a pom-pom. Find the middle of the pom-pom, moving the yarn strands out of the way to easily see the center. Apply a large amount of hot glue to the center—you want it to hold well to the dowel.

5 Insert the dowel into the pom-pom. Push the dowel into the pom-pom and hold it together tightly to allow the hot glue to cool. Make sure not to push the dowel all the way through the pom-pom.

6 **Decorate the pennant.** Cut out shapes, letters, or other designs from another piece of felt. An electric cutter or precut felt letters can be used to get more-precise shapes and letters. Hot-glue the felt pieces to the pennant.

7 **Add embellishments.** Tie pieces of yarn or ribbon to the dowel. Add glitter, sequins, or other embellishments if desired. To ensure that the ribbon or yarn doesn't slide down the dowel, put a dot of hot glue on the back of the dowel, then adhere the ribbons to the glue.

Wand

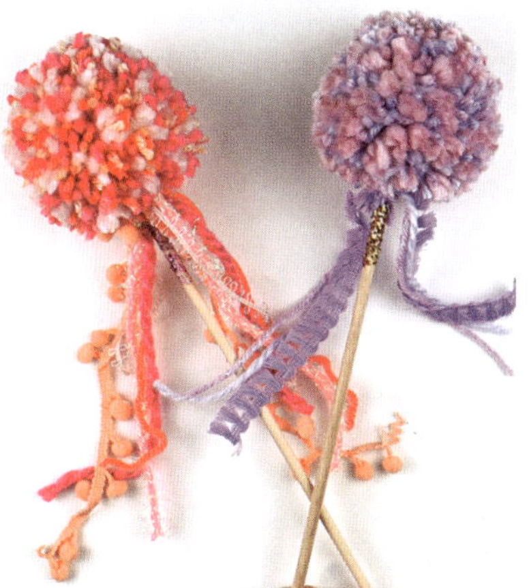

1 **Apply glue to the dowel.** Using a paintbrush, apply a few inches of school glue to the end of a dowel, leaving 1" (2.5 cm) clean at the top. The top will be covered by a pom-pom, so no school glue is needed there.

2 **Sprinkle with glitter.** Cover the wet glue in glitter. Make sure to sprinkle over a paper plate or surface that can collect the unused glitter. Allow the glue to dry completely before adding the pom-pom.

3 **Glue the pom-pom to the dowel.** Repeat steps 4–5 from the Pennant by hot-gluing the dowel to the inside of the pom-pom. Use a large amount of hot glue to make sure the pom-pom is secure. Add embellishments such as yarn and ribbon to the dowel.

THE COLOR MEDITATION DECK
The Secret Lives of Color

materials + tools

- Yarn
  - Medium-weight acrylic
  - 11 colors
  - About 10–17 yards (9.1–15.5 m) of each color or about 140 yards (128 m) total
- **24" x 48" (61 x 122 cm) pegboard**
- **Pencil**
- **Yarn needle**
- **Scissors**
- **Tape**
- **Pegboard-grid template on page 163**

CROSS-STITCH PEGBOARD

Late nights are often when creative ideas hit me. I was lying in bed one night thinking about what I could do for my next craft project, when I thought, "How can I make a cross-stitch pattern on a large scale?" Thinking through the different options for materials that could work as a large cross-stitch canvas, pegboard seemed like a winner! After making a few pieces, I was even lucky enough to have one of my pegboard cross-stitch patterns featured in *Mollie Makes Magazine*. While a traditional, wood-like pegboard is always a great option for this project, you can now find plastic pegboard as well, which is a little less messy, since it doesn't flake off while pulling the yarn through. Any size of pegboard can be used for this project—cut your design down to fit the space you have. These pieces add unique art to your home and can fill those hard-to-style wall spaces.

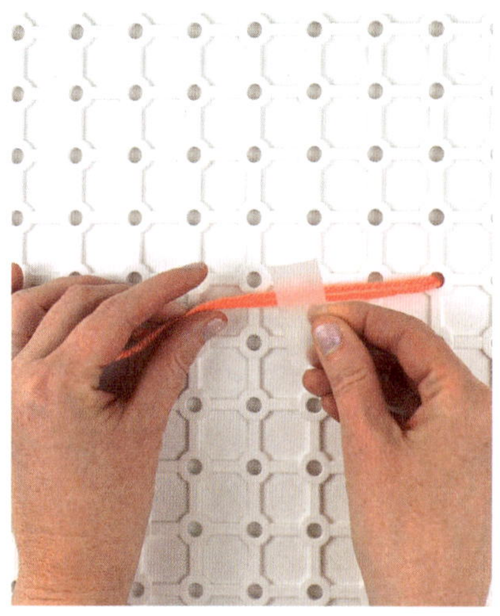

1 Find the center of the pegboard. Count the squares along the width and length to find the center square. Make a small mark with a pencil in the center of that square. The pattern will be worked starting from the center and working outward.

2 String the yarn needle. Cut about 24"–48" (61–122 cm) of the first color of yarn. Double up the yarn on the needle so that each stitch is made of two strands of yarn. Don't make a knot at the bottom of the yarn—this helps reduce bulkiness on the back.

3 Tape the yarn ends to the back of the pegboard. String the yarn through the bottom left center hole from back to front, then tape the ends of the yarn down to secure them. Make sure the tape doesn't cover any holes. Clear tape works best.

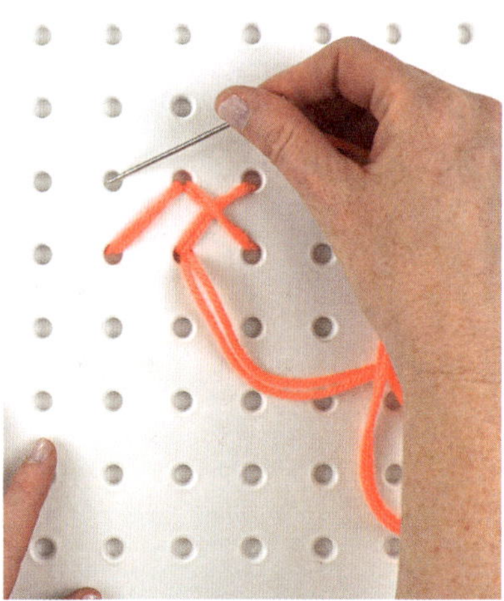

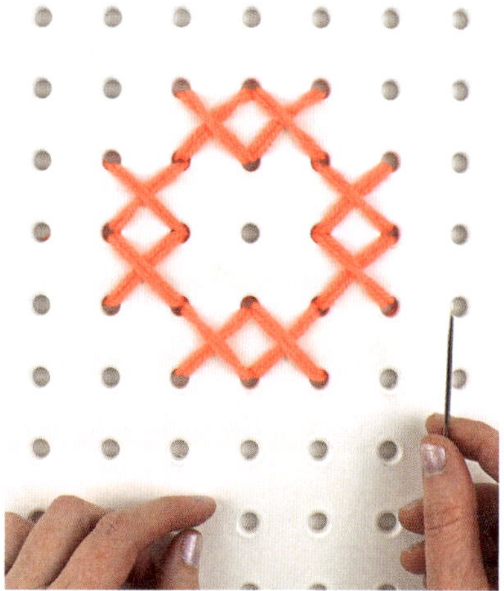

4 Make half stitches. With the yarn on the front, stitch into the hole above and to the right of the initial hole. This will make half a stitch. Repeat with any other stitches of the same color in the same row. It's easiest to work across the row from left to right.

5 Complete the stitches. Now working from right to left, go back over each half stitch to complete each "X" from bottom right to top left. Finish every stitch in the row. When you're done with the section, end with the needle and yarn on the backside of the pegboard.

6 Complete the first color. It is easiest to work one color in one section at a time rather than constantly switching colors. Since this pattern is made up of small sections of diamonds, finish one entire diamond in one color before moving on.

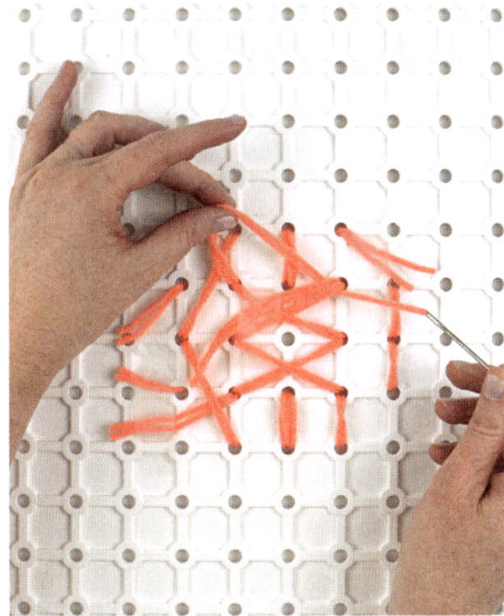

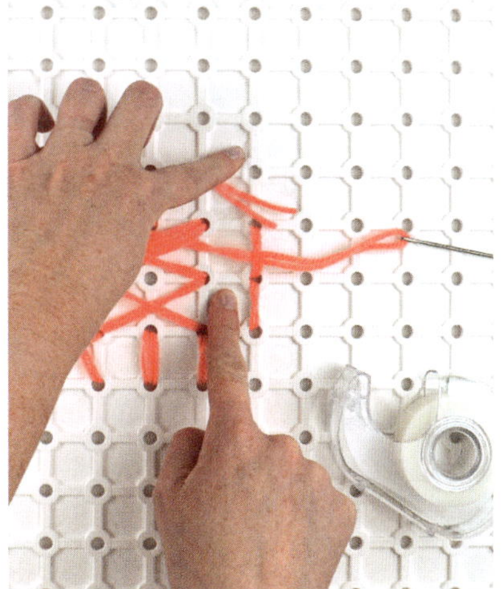

7 Feed the needle through several stitches on the back. When finishing with a color, feed the needle through a few stitches on the backside to secure the yarn. Knots won't work well, since they can fit through the pegboard holes and will make the back bulky.

8 Tape the yarn ends on the back. To make the yarn more secure, tape the ends that were just fed under the stitches on the back. As a rule, tape all ends of yarn whenever starting or ending a stitch.

9 Cut off the needle. The needle will still be strung on the yarn, since the yarn was doubled up. It will need to be cut off the yarn every time the yarn needs to be changed. Trim any long excess yarn left on the backside.

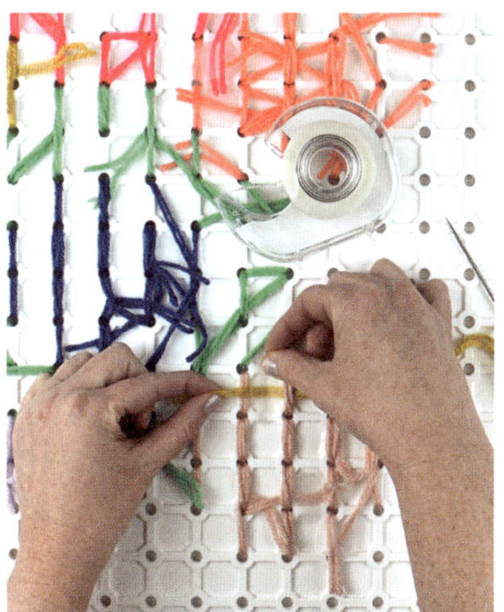

10 Start a new color. Double up the yarn on the needle like before and feed the needle through a few stitches on the backside. Now that there are a few stitches on the board, the yarn can be secured under several stitches when starting a new color. You should still add tape though.

11 Secure the ends with tape. When finished with the next color, tape the ends in place like before. Always tape the ends to hold the yarn in place! Repeat steps 2–9 with each new color to complete the design.

tip

It helps to prop up the pegboard against a wall or table while stitching—if it's flat, the board has to be lifted for every stitch.

materials + tools

- Yarn
  - Light, medium, or bulky weight
  - 6 colors
  - About 25 yards (23 m) total
- **Metal grid, fencing, or chicken wire measuring 12" x 24" (30 x 61 cm) or 24 squares by 48 squares—each square measures ½" (1.5 cm)**
- **Wire cutters**
- **Needlenose pliers**
- **Work gloves**
- **Wire-grid template on page 165**

STITCHED WIRE GRID

This project may require you to skip the craft store and head to the home improvement store instead! Metal grids, chicken wire, and metal fencing are typically not used for craft projects, but they lend themselves beautifully to stitched art. Because the geometric grid mimics cross-stitch fabric or canvas, yarn can be stitched on the grid by wrapping it around the wires. The contrast between the soft yarn and the industrial metal creates an unexpected but lovely piece of art. Fencing and metal grids come in many different heights and widths, so you can make this piece as large or small as you would like. The pattern repeats, so it can easily be adjusted for a larger or smaller size of metal grid.

STITCHED WIRE GRID

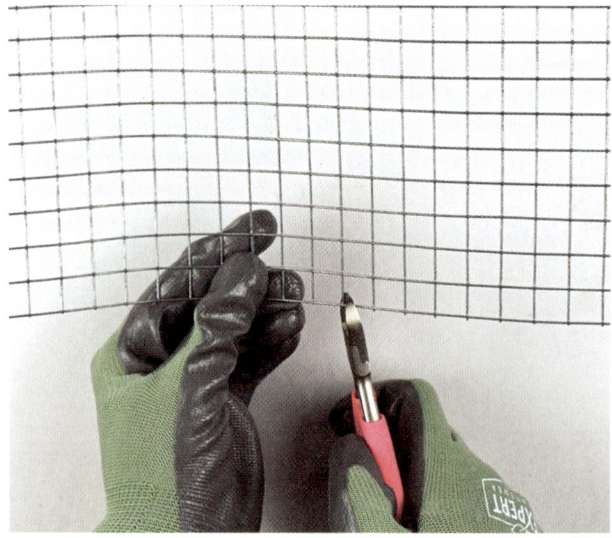

1 Cut the wire grid. Wear work gloves to protect yourself from sharp edges. Use wire cutters to cut the desired width or number of squares across. Once cut, if there are any sharp edges, use pliers to bend the wire into a curved edge. Always use caution when working with metal.

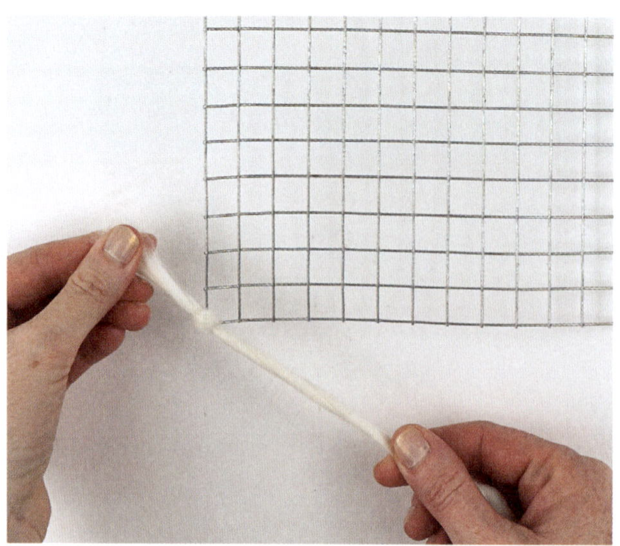

2 Tie the yarn onto the grid. If the grid is sharp, keep your gloves on while working. Double-knot the first color of yarn to the corner of the grid. The end of the yarn can be hidden at the end or left out, depending on your preference.

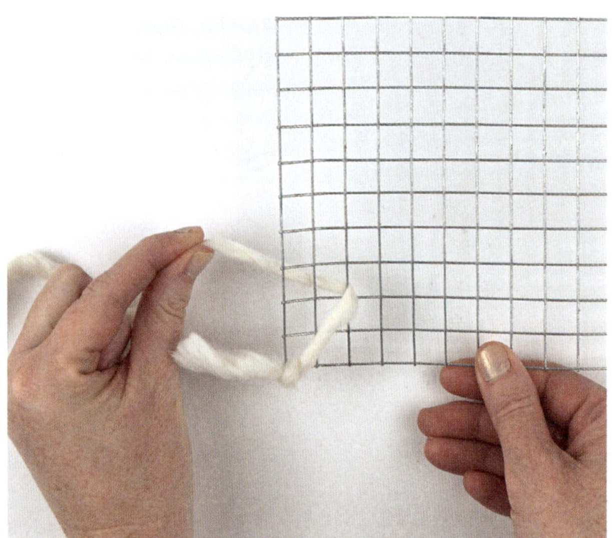

3 Begin following the pattern. To make a diagonal line, string the yarn up across the desired square and diagonally insert it into the square directly next to that square. Pull through. If you're crossing multiple squares (as done here), you can skip directly to your target.

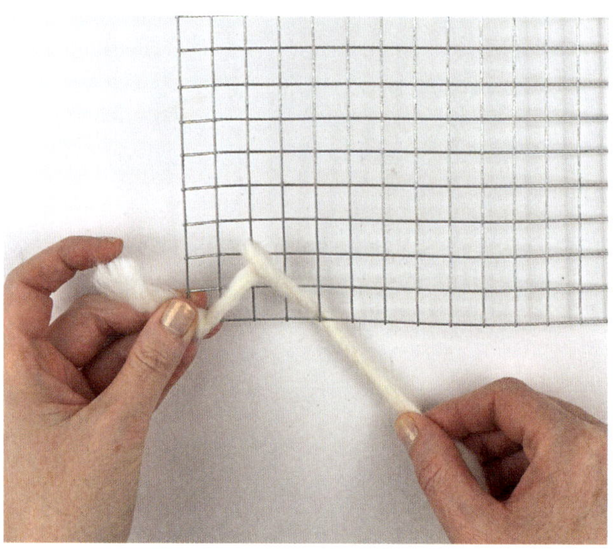

4 Move to the next square. Depending on the location of the next square, wrap the yarn around the wire nearby so that it is aiming in the correct direction. For example, to move down and diagonally to the right, wrap the yarn around the wire from right to left.

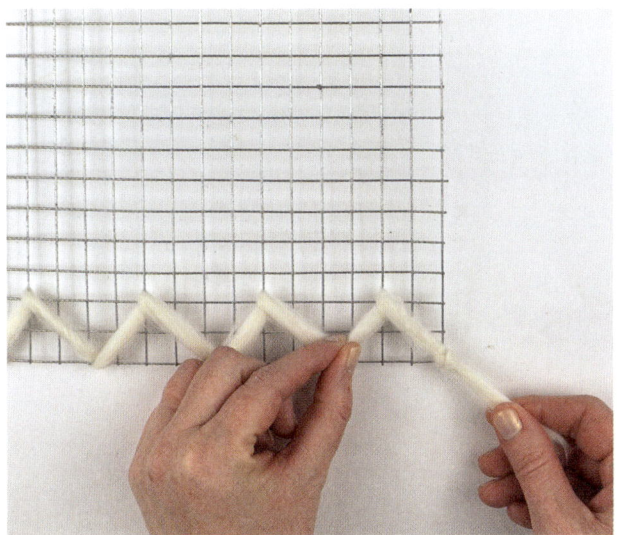

5 **Continue the pattern across the grid.** Always keep the next stitch in mind as you work, because this will determine how you should wrap the yarn around the wire. At the end of a color, tie the yarn to the grid with another double knot.

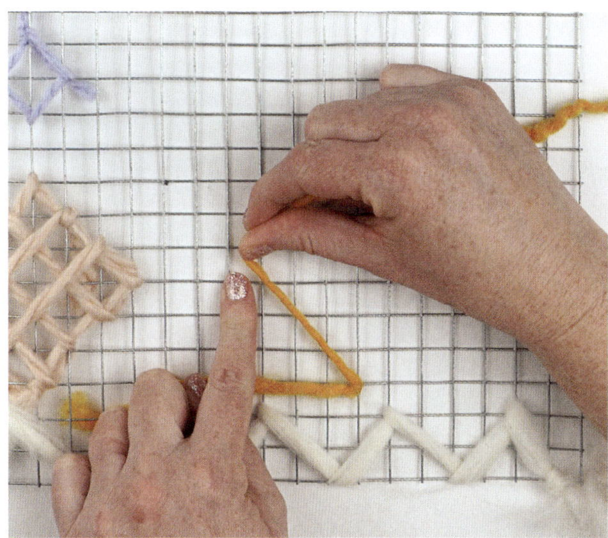

6 **Begin the interior stitching.** With most diagonal stitches, the yarn will be inserted into the square that is one diagonal from the desired square, as if continuing the line upward. This will help you cover the correct number of squares with the stitch. For nondiagonal lines, insert the yarn into the square directly above, below, right of, or left of the desired square.

7 **Hot-glue the yarn ends to the backside.** For a more polished look, the yarn ends can be hot-glued to the wire on the back. Hide the ends under the designs so that they are less visible from the front. For a messy-chic look, though, the ends can be left loose.

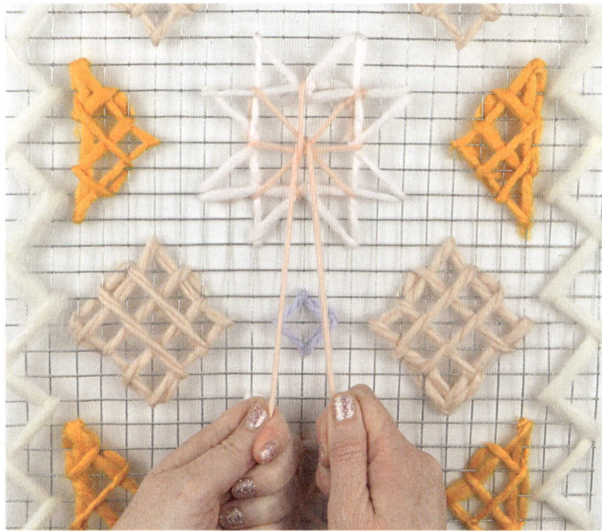

8 **Tie loose strands of yarn to the front.** If desired, yarn can be added to the front to add a tassel-like effect. Double-knot it directly onto the wire. Add strands of yarn to the bottom as well for extra embellishment.

Lucky You

WOVEN YARN ART

materials + tools

- Yarn
  - Medium to bulky weight (keep the weights fairly similar)
  - As many colors as desired
  - For a 9" x 11" (23 x 28 cm) frame: about 35 yards (32 m)
- **Picture frame (raised or floating varieties work well)**
- **Hot-glue gun**
- **Scissors**
- **Clear packing tape or regular tape**
- **Yarn needle (optional)**

A few years ago, I saw a beautiful piece of art on a home décor website. The piece was made from natural fibers that were woven together and mounted on a wooden frame. I loved the look, but at almost $200, I didn't love the price. I thought there must be a way to create the piece at home and in a much more affordable way. This project is my take on that art piece, but instead of using natural fibers, I used yarn. I was also able to use colors of my choosing that went with my décor instead of the colors on the expensive version. While woven art can be created on a loom, this project uses hot glue and a picture frame. No loom experience necessary! A grid art piece can be made with any size of frame and with any color combos.

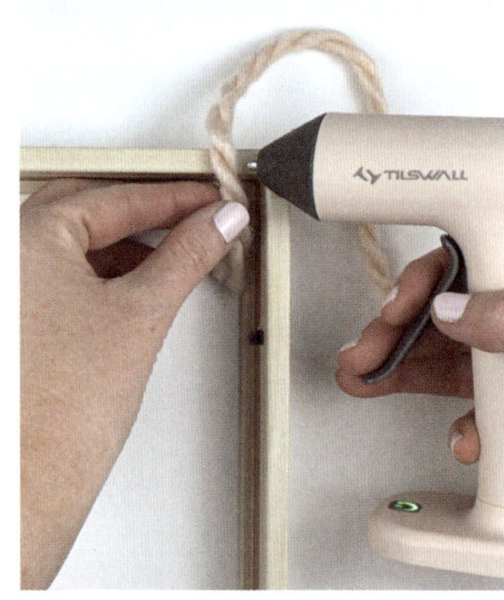

1 Remove the glass from the frame. Take off the back of the frame and remove the glass and any additional pieces. No mat or backing will be needed. Also remove any pieces attached to the frame that are used for holding the backing in place.

2 Hot-glue the yarn to the frame. Cut a piece of yarn longer than the length of the frame. Turn the frame to the backside and put a dot of hot glue next to the top right corner. Stick the end of the piece of yarn to the hot glue with a short tail toward the inside of the frame and the length going out away from the frame.

3 Wrap the yarn around the frame. Now wrap the yarn around the top edge to the front of the frame, down the length of the frame, and back around the bottom edge to the back of the frame again. Then hot-glue the yarn to the backside.

4 Continue, then trim. Continue hot-gluing pieces of yarn in this manner all the way across, leaving some space in between each strand. Make sure each strand has its little tail on each end. Then trim the tails, but not too short, or you won't be able to secure them in the next step.

5 Tape the ends. Using clear packing tape cut in half lengthwise or regular tape, apply tape to the inside of the frame to hold the tails in place. This will help with fraying and will make the piece more secure. Add hot glue to the tape if it has trouble sticking.

6 Hot-glue a piece of yarn to the empty edge. Still working on the backside, put a dot of hot glue next to the top right corner on the empty edge. Stick a new piece of yarn to it, just like you've been doing, with a small tail toward the inside.

7 **Begin weaving.** Turn the frame to the front, then weave the new piece of yarn under and over the strands of yarn already on the frame. You can use a yarn needle to do this if desired, but your hands work well too. Hot-glue this yarn to the back as you've been doing.

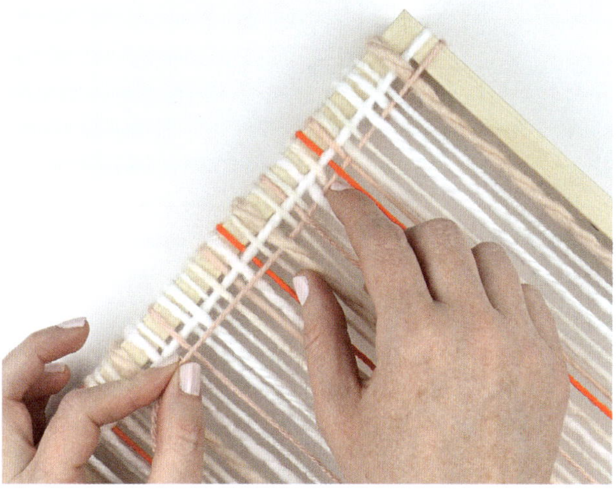

8 **Alternate the weaving direction.** Add a second strand and weave it, but this time, alternate the direction from the first strand by going over and then under. Continue to alternate the direction of the weaving for each new strand to complete the whole frame.

9 **Trim and tape the ends.** Like you did for the first two edges, trim the yarn ends, leaving just enough to fold onto the inside of the frame. Secure the ends with tape and more hot glue if necessary. Make sure no ends can be seen from the front.

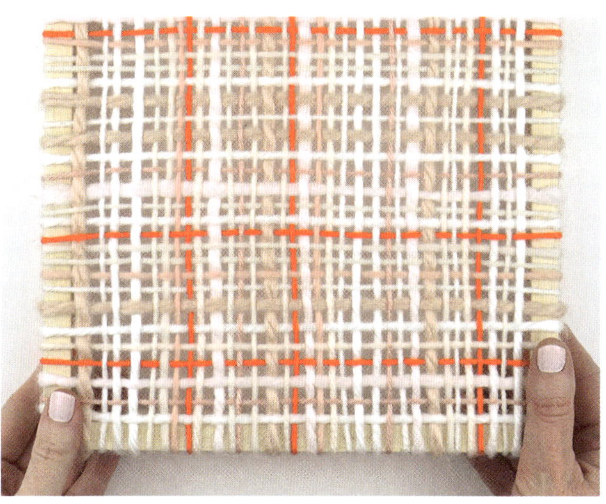

10 **Display!** If desired, add a picture hanger or a piece of yarn to the back of the frame for hanging. This woven design can also be simply propped on a shelf or leaned against a wall.

POM-POM CACTI

I like to think of myself as a plant person. I have quite a few live plants around my home, and, in the warm months, I grow as many flowers as I can in my garden. Even though I love my plants, caring for them can be a little demanding. Each plant needs a different amount of water, light, or fertilizer. With a pom-pom cactus, though, you never have to worry about watering, weather, or light at all! These cute succulents can go anywhere in the house: on a bookshelf, a windowsill, or a nightstand. They also make a darling gift. I used to sell these in my shop, and they were one of my bestsellers!

materials + tools

- **Yarn**
    - Light, medium, or bulky weight
    - Green yarn for cacti:
        - For a 3 ½" (9 cm) pom-pom: about 42 yards (38.4 m) of medium-weight yarn*
    - Bright-colored yarn for flower(s):
        - For a 1" (2.5 cm) pom-pom: about 8 yards (7.3 m) of medium-weight yarn*
- **Large pom-pom maker with a diameter slightly larger than the mouth of the flowerpot**
- **Small pom-pom maker**
- **Embroidery scissors**
- **Trimming scissors**
- **Small flowerpots (papier-mâché, terra-cotta, or plastic all work well)**
- **Hot-glue gun**
- **Small, colorful pom-poms for embellishing**

*Yarn amounts will vary depending on the weight of yarn and size of pom-pom maker.

1 Make a large pom-pom. Make one large pom-pom whose finished diameter is slightly larger than the opening of the flowerpot. Combine different shades of green for a textured effect.

2 Make small pom-poms. A small plastic pom-pom maker or a small cardboard maker can be used to make these. These small pom-poms will be the flowers on the cacti, so bright colors work best.

3 Apply hot glue to the inside of the flowerpot. Apply a layer of hot glue all around the inside rim of the flowerpot, working quickly so that the glue doesn't harden. Don't skimp on the glue—apply a thick layer.

4 Add the cactus pom-pom. Stick the green pom-pom inside the flowerpot, leaving over half of the pom-pom showing above the rim. Be careful not to push the pom-pom down too far. Hold it for a few seconds to allow the glue to harden.

5 Glue the embellishments. Using a hot-glue gun, apply glue to the small pom-poms and stick them to the green pom-pom. Hold them for a few seconds to secure. Continue embellishing as desired. Felt flowers or mini pom-poms can also be added for variety!

FLORAL TOTE BAG

In my garden, I have a collection of dahlias, zinnias, tulips, roses, hydrangeas, and peonies. I walk through my yard each day during their blooming season to see the new blooms that have popped up. Unfortunately, I live in a state that gets quite cold during the winter, so I get to enjoy the fresh flowers from my yard for only a few months each year. In the cold months, I like to create yarn flowers to bring the cheerfulness of fresh flowers into my home. Flower looms have been around for years, and, if you are lucky enough, you may find a vintage flower loom in an antique or thrift shop. If you can't find a vintage one, new ones are available online. Round looms, like those used to make crochet hats, also work great for making these flowers. Round looms are easier to find, and they are less expensive than flower looms, but either type of loom can be used for this project.

materials + tools

- **Yarn**
  - Medium, bulky, or super-bulky weight
  - At least 2 colors, but as many as desired
  - For a 5 ½" (14 cm) round loom: about 5 yards (4.6 m) of bulky acrylic yarn per flower
  - For the centers: about 12" (31 cm) of bulky acrylic yarn
- **5 ½" (14 cm) round loom or flower loom**
- **Yarn needle with large eye**
- **Fabric stiffener (optional)**
- **Tote bag**
- **Hot-glue gun**

1 **Wrap the yarn around a peg on the loom.** Holding on to a long end of yarn on the backside of the loom, wind the yarn up through the center and around the outside of a peg. Then find the peg directly across from the first peg and wrap the yarn across and around the outside of that peg.

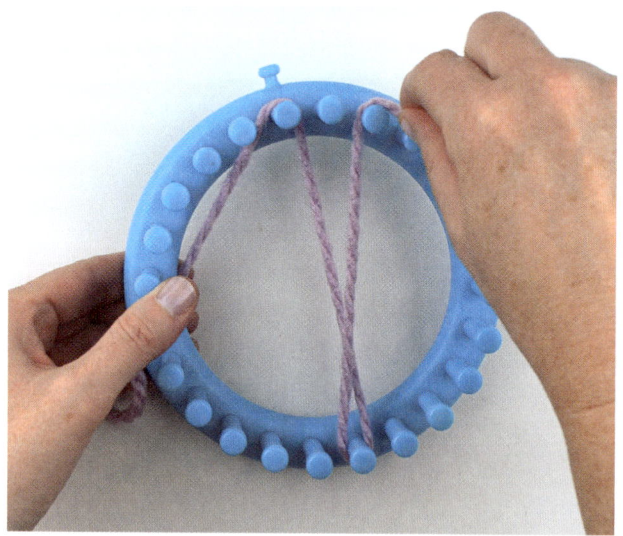

2 **Zigzag the yarn across the loom.** Bring the yarn back across to the top, skip the peg to the right or left of the first peg, and wrap around that next peg. For a fuller flower, don't skip any pegs. We are making a zigzag pattern across the loom. Keep holding the tail end.

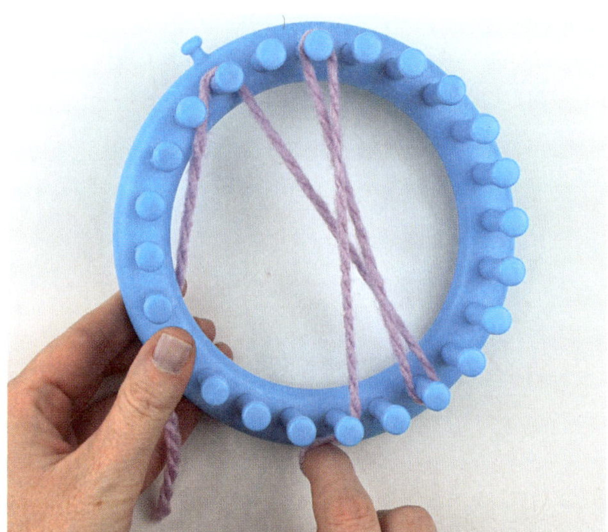

3 **Wind the yarn around the fourth peg.** Skip a peg at the bottom like you did at the top, so that the yarn is going directly across again. Follow this pattern of skip one peg, wind one peg (or not skipping any pegs if you're making a fuller flower).

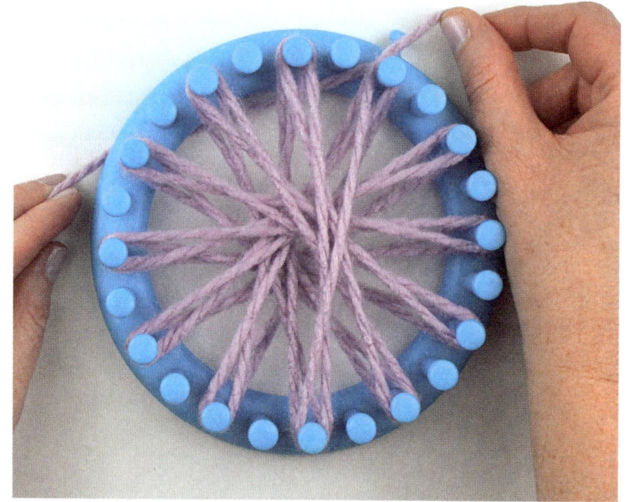

4 **Continue weaving back and forth all the way around.** At some point, the yarn should end up back at the first peg. For a thicker flower, go around the loom in the same manner twice. I prefer making my flowers doubled up this way.

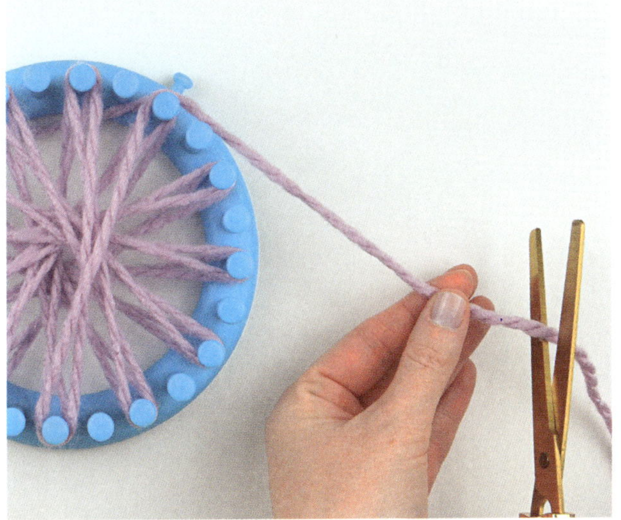

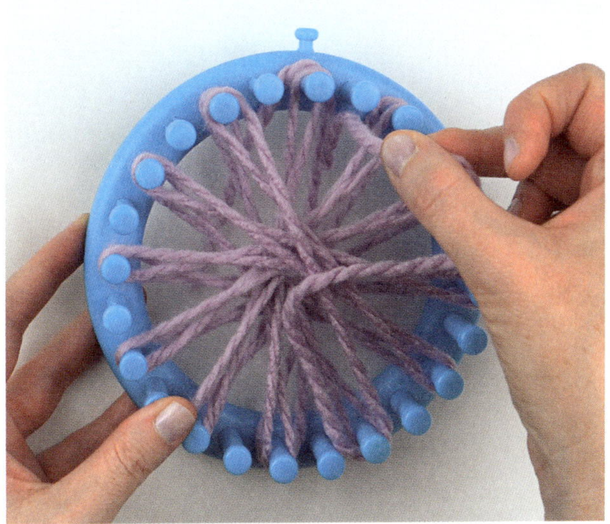

5 Cut the yarn. The newly cut end will be used for tying the flower together, so leave it long. You will trim it down later. Continue to hold the other end at the start of the loom (or at least make sure it's secure, as I've done here).

6 Feed the long end from the front side to the back. Poke the yarn through the weaving to the backside of the loom. Try to feed the end into the center in between the wrapped pegs, rather than through a wrapped peg.

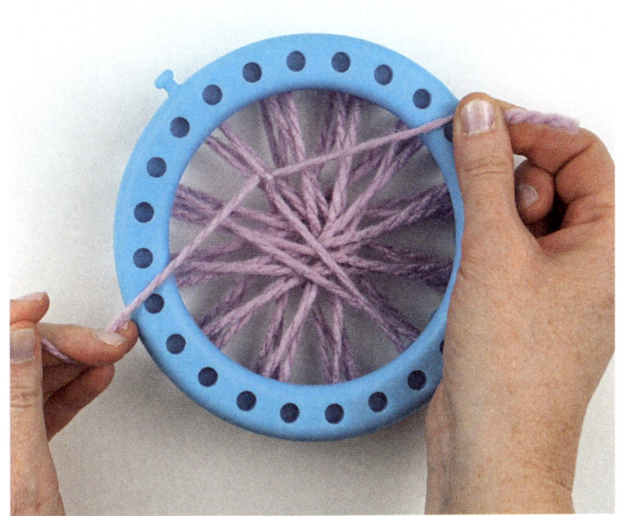

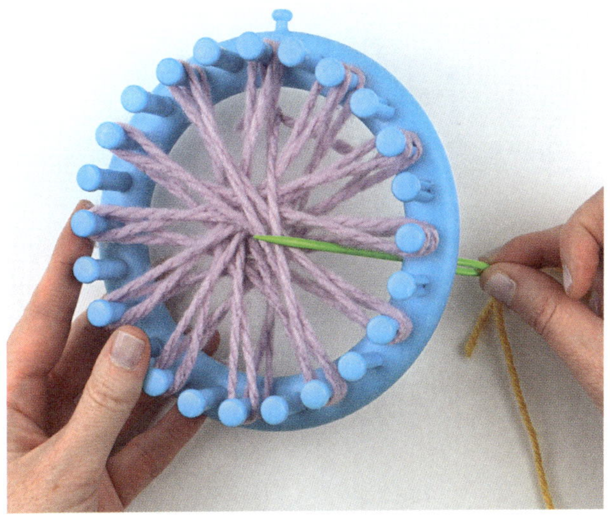

7 Tie the two ends in a knot. While still holding on to the first end, knot the two ends together tightly. Make sure the knot is on the backside of the flower and loom. Trim the ends, leaving about ½" (1.5 cm) of yarn on each end.

8 Stitch the center of the flower. String a yarn needle with a different color of yarn and insert the needle in between the existing strands of yarn on the loom from the backside to the front. Leave a long end, holding the end to keep it from pulling through.

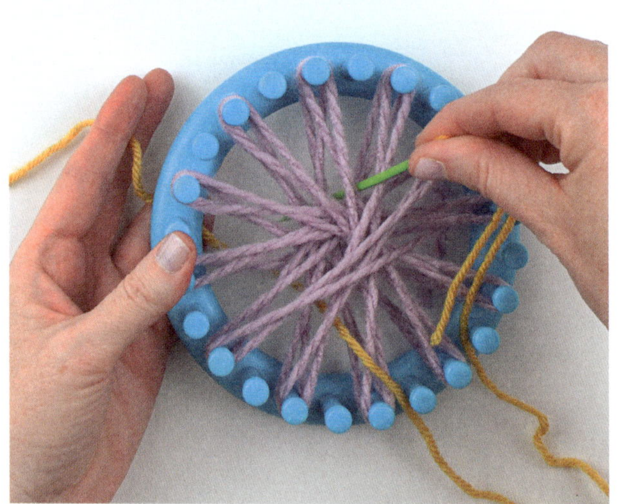

9 **Insert the needle into the empty space above or below.** While still holding on to the end, insert the needle into the gap directly across the center of the loom from where you initially pulled the yarn up through.

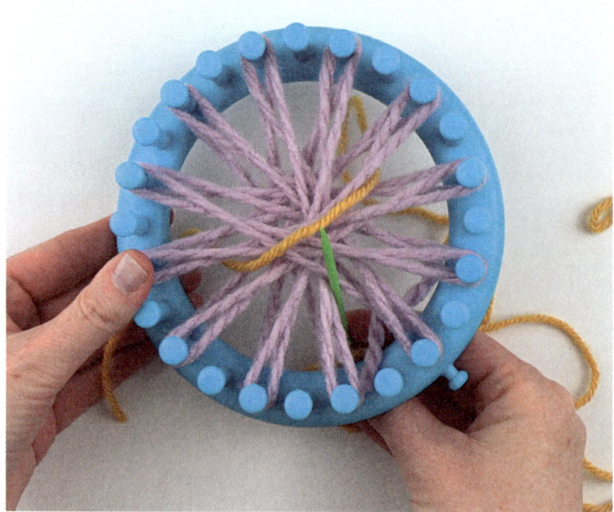

10 **Insert the needle from the backside again.** Choose a different gap on the backside, bring the needle up through to the front, and insert it into the gap directly across the center again. Continue cinching the center like this by making sure that the center string is pulled through every gap in the flower.

11 **Pull the ends of the center string to tighten.** Make sure all gaps have been stitched—if any gaps are skipped, the petals may come apart. Then, with both ends of the yarn on the backside, pull the center tight so that the flower stays together.

12 **Knot the center strings on the back.** Tie the center together tightly. Trim the long ends of the yarn. Leave about ½" (1.5 cm) on the ends so that they aren't very visible from the front.

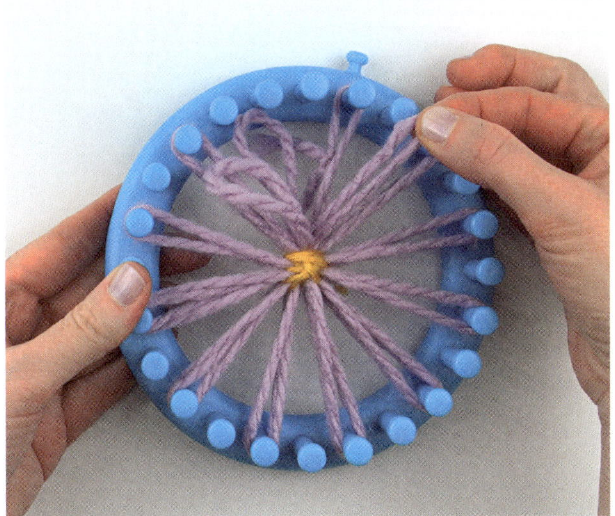

13 **Remove the flower from the loom.** Carefully remove each petal from the pegs. If desired, you could use a small hook to remove the yarn from each peg. Usually, though, the petals will come off the pegs fairly easily by hand.

14 **Spray the flower with fabric stiffener.** This step is optional, but it helps the flower not to be as floppy. Protect your workspace before spraying to avoid getting the spray on furniture. Allow the stiffener to dry completely, according to the manufacturer's instructions.

15 **Hot-glue the flowers to the tote bag.** Depending on the thickness of the bag's fabric, insert a piece of cardboard or plastic inside the bag so that the glue doesn't seep through. Apply hot glue to the center and a few petals of each flower to help secure them.

tip

Stack several flowers in the same or different sizes for an even-fuller flower.

BIG HEART

Jumbo yarn is perfect for large-scale projects. This big heart requires only yarn, a cardboard box, and lots and lots of hot glue! I filmed a television segment once where I crafted a giant yarn rainbow. I pieced together two pieces of foam core and hot-glued chunky yarn to it. After the segment aired, I hung that giant rainbow in my daughter's room above her bed. It made a great faux headboard! This big heart uses the same technique as that rainbow. If hearts aren't your thing, you could cut any shape out of cardboard to cover in yarn—stars, a letter of the alphabet, an animal shape, or a large bow all are possibilities that use this simple technique. Just make sure you have lots of hot-glue sticks on hand before you begin!

materials + tools

- Yarn
  - Bulky, super-bulky, and jumbo weights in various textures
  - At least 1 color, but as many colors as desired
  - Amount depends on the size of the heart
- **Cardboard or foam board cut into a large heart**
- **Hot-glue gun**

1 Start hot-gluing yarn to the heart. Cut a heart out of cardboard. Then, starting along the outside edge, hot-glue a strand of yarn to the cardboard. Try to cover the edge with the yarn so that the cardboard doesn't show. Hot-glue the yarn all the way around the heart.

2 Hot-glue another row of yarn. Making sure that no cardboard shows between the strands, glue another round of yarn to the heart. Glue in small sections at a time, so that the glue doesn't cool more quickly than you can work. If the glue is too cool, the yarn will not stick to it. Continue gluing yarn for several more rounds.

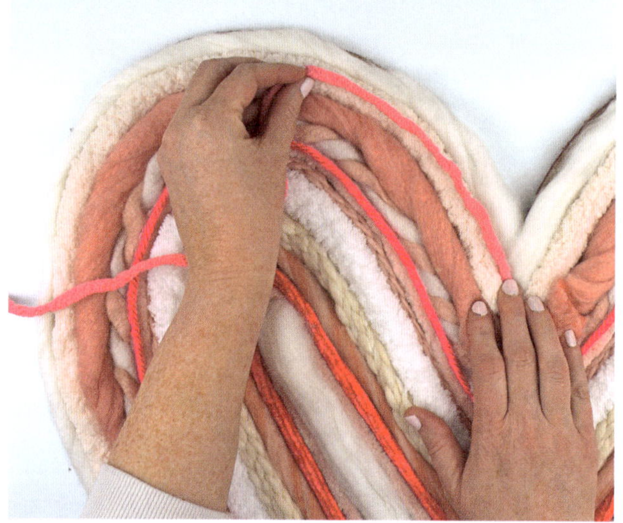

3 Fill in the center with the same yarn. To avoid having a "V" shape in the center of the heart, stop making rounds while the center still looks like a heart shape. Use one kind of yarn to fill in that whole space. But, if you prefer, you can continue as before by changing yarn each round.

4 Add additional yarn on top of the jumbo yarn. For extra dimension and detail, glue smaller thicknesses of yarn directly to the top of the jumbo yarn already glued down. Other embellishments, such as pom-pom trim or tinsel, can be added as well.

tip

For extra-large projects, two pieces of cardboard or foam board can be taped together to make a bigger shape.

materials + tools

- Yarn
  - Medium-weight acrylic
  - At least 1 color, but as many as desired
  - For a 2" (5 cm) pom-pom: about 18 yards (16.5 m) per pom-pom
  - For a 1" (2.5 cm) pom-pom: about 8 yards (7.3 m) per pom-pom
  - For a large tassel: about 12 yards (11 m)
- About 20 yards (18.3 m) of embroidery floss
- Ruler
- Scissors
- Paper straws
- Small or medium pom-pom makers (or both)
- Embroidery scissors
- Large circular punch (optional)
- Tissue paper
- Large beads
- Yarn needle
- Washi tape
- Embroidery hoop insert or macrame hoop
- Tassel maker

CHANDELIER

Several years ago, I was invited to demonstrate a project for a craft segment on a local TV show. The project they asked me to make was a pajaki, which is a traditional paper chandelier made in Poland. Pajakis are typically made using straws and paper and are traditionally vibrant and colorful. They are used for celebrations and during the winter months, which I think is a perfect way to brighten up a cold winter. Often, flowers are made of paper and attached to the chandelier, but I knew that pom-poms could be a perfect substitution for flowers. I also knew that my version had to include a yarn tassel at the bottom! I have made several versions of these pajakis since that craft segment, but I change up the colors, size, and design each time. These chandeliers are darling décor for parties and can also be hung in a bedroom or craft room. Use supplies you have on hand, like beads, felt, fabric, and ribbon, to make your chandelier unique!

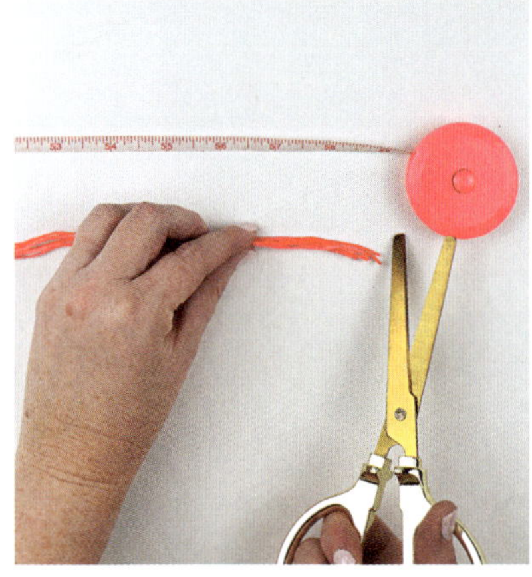

1 Cut the floss. Use a ruler to measure 60" (152 cm) lengths of embroidery floss. Depending on the size of your embroidery hoop, cut a total of six to ten strands of the floss. I used six strands for a hoop that measures 12" (31 cm) in diameter. The more strands you have, the more detailed and dense the chandelier will be.

2 Cut up paper straws. For smaller embroidery hoops, cut pieces about 1 ½"–2" (4–5 cm) in length. For larger hoops, cut pieces about 3" (7.5 cm) in length. For my chandelier, I used about 80 pieces of straws that measured about 1 ½" (4 cm) each. Larger, sharp scissors work best for this.

3 Make the pom-poms. Using your pom-pom maker, acrylic yarn, and scissors, make several small and medium pom-poms. The number of pom-poms will depend on your preference. I used 12 pom-poms in my chandelier.

4 Punch or cut circles out of tissue paper. Tissue paper can be layered to cut through several sheets at once. Punch or cut about 100 circles of about 1 ½"–2" (4–5 cm) in diameter. More circles can always be punched later if you run out.

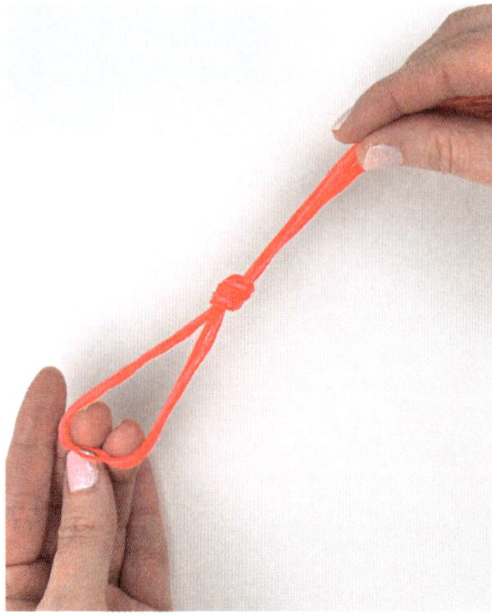

5 Tie a hanging loop in the floss. Line up all the strands of floss evenly, then fold the bunch in the middle. Tie a knot with all the strands of floss a few inches down from the fold to create a hanging loop. If desired, slide a bead up the floss to the knot.

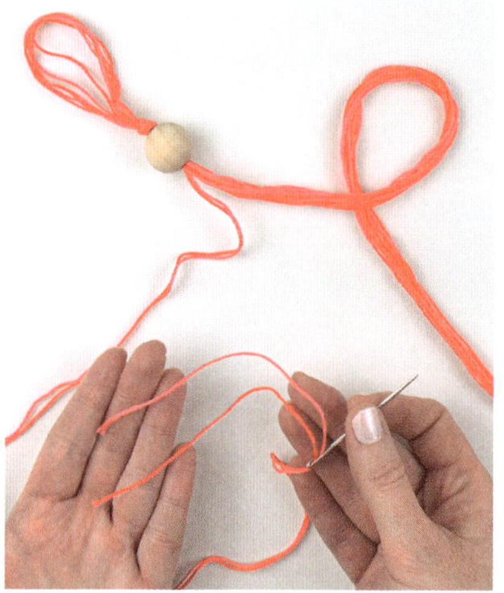

6 Thread the yarn needle. Hold two strands of embroidery floss and thread the yarn needle with them. Make sure both pieces of floss go through the eye, since both pieces will be used at the same time for the top portion of the chandelier.

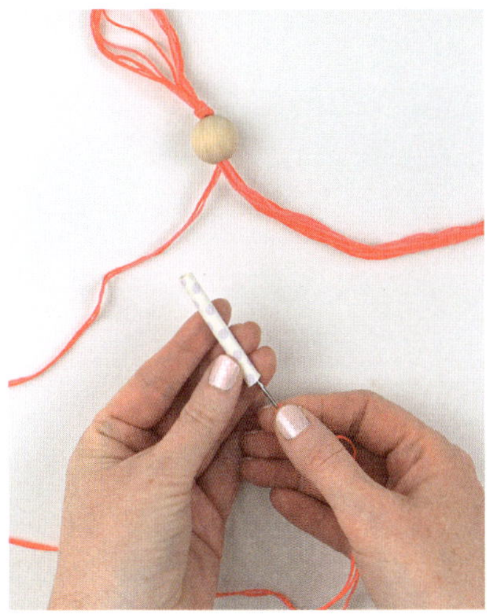

7 Begin stringing with a straw piece. String one straw piece through the needle and both strands of floss. Push it all the way up to the top of the strands. Straws are a good first item for stringing because they help keep the floss from tangling at the top.

8 String on tissue-paper circles. Layer two or three tissue-paper circles and crinkle them up a bit. This gives added dimension and makes them fuller. Use the needle to poke a hole through the center of the stack, then slide the stack all the way up to the bottom of the first straw piece.

9 Continue the stringing pattern. Continue to string items onto the floss by alternating one straw piece and one stack of tissue-paper circles until about 9" (23 cm) of the floss is filled. End the pattern with a straw piece. Below the final straw, add a little washi-tape flag to hold everything in place.

10 Repeat steps 6–9. For the remaining pieces of embroidery floss, pair strands up and string them with the same pattern. At the end, if you started with six strands doubled up (so, 12 working strands) like I did, you will have six sections total.

11 Lay the sections over the hoop. Lay your six straw sections over the embroidery hoop to get them to be evenly spaced. Try to make them as even as possible. Washi tape can be used to hold the sections to the hoop if desired.

12 Tie one section to the hoop. Take the two strands of embroidery floss at the bottom of one section and tie them together around the hoop. (Place one strand to the inside and one to the outside, then make a knot.) The knot should sit at the bottom of the hoop.

13 Tie all the sections to the hoop. Continue tying the two strands of floss of each section to the hoop all the way around, maintaining your even spacing. If the sections are not evenly spaced after tying them on, carefully slide them along the hoop as needed to even them out.

14 Start stringing one strand of floss. Unlike for the completed top sections, the lower sections will use only one strand of floss each, so you'll have double the number of strands. Choose one strand of floss and begin adding straws, pom-poms, beads, and tissue paper. Fill about 6 ½" (16 cm) and end with a straw.

15 Match the pattern. Select one strand of floss from the two strands in the next set and string this strand just like you did in step 14, matching that pattern of straws, pom-poms, beads, and tissue paper.

16 Connect the finished strands. Hold the ends of your two finished strands together and thread both strands of floss through the needle. By combining two strands again, the chandelier will narrow back down toward the bottom.

17 String the bottommost section of floss. Add beads, straws, and tissue paper to this combined bottommost section of floss, ending with a straw. Make this final section about 3" (7.5 cm) long. Attach washi tape to secure the bottom. There should be a few inches of floss left at the bottom.

18 Repeat steps 14–17. Continue stringing individual strands of floss, then pairing them with the strand adjacent to them. String every strand of floss all the way around the hoop, securing each final section at the bottom.

19 Tie a knot at the bottom. Gather all the strands of floss around the bottom and tie a knot. There will not be much floss remaining, but there should be just enough for a knot. This step brings the chandelier to life and gives it shape.

20 Add a tassel to the bottom knot. Using a tassel maker or piece of cardboard, make a large tassel. Feed a piece of yarn through the top of the tassel, then use that piece of yarn to tie the tassel to the bottom knot, securing it to the chandelier.

tip

For larger, more-detailed chandeliers, add more floss strands at the beginning. Keep each floss section close to the same length so that the chandelier hangs evenly.

CREATE

materials + tools

- Yarn
  - Medium-weight acrylic
  - At least 1 color, but as many as desired
  - About 15 yards (13.7 m) (depends on size of bowl)
- **Two identical cereal or smaller bowls**
- **Plastic wrap**
- **Paper plate**
- **Water**
- **School glue**
- **Small bowl for glue**
- **Spoon for mixing**
- **Scissors**

YARN DISH

When you have a lot of craft supplies, you need a lot of storage options. I love to have little bowls to collect little items in my craft room, and yarn bowls are a perfect way to add some color and character. Since they do have some open spaces in them, these bowls are best for items like rolls of washi tape, spools of thread, or pom-poms rather than tiny items. These bowls use a technique similar to papier-mâché, where a glue solution is applied to yarn, then allowed to harden. Note that this project does take a few days to ensure that the dish has dried entirely. Be patient! The end result is really fun. It is a bit of a messy project, but sometimes it is fun to get a little messy. Kids could easily do this project as well. Just keep some paper towels handy!

1 Cover the cereal bowl with plastic wrap. Set one of the cereal bowls upside down on a paper plate. Wrap a piece of plastic wrap around the bowl, covering the whole outside of the bowl and around the rim to the inside.

2 Pour glue in a small bowl. Pour school glue into a small bowl. This project uses quite a bit of glue. More glue can always be added as needed later, and excess can be emptied back into the glue container.

3 Add water to the glue. To make the glue a little easier to work with, add a small amount of water to it. Stir the mixture with a spoon to get the water incorporated. The glue should not be incredibly runny—it should be just a little thinner than the pure glue.

4 Soak a strand of yarn in the glue. Cut a fairly long strand of yarn and add it to the bowl of glue. Cover the yarn completely with glue. The yarn should be saturated, so make sure all of it is coated well. Try to keep the yarn from getting tangled in the bowl.

5 Lay the yarn over the bottom of the bowl. As you start to pull the yarn from the glue bowl, squeeze some of the excess glue out of the strand—it should not be dripping. Use one hand to lay the yarn on the bowl and the other to remove excess glue as you go.

6 Cover the bottom of the bowl with yarn. Add the yarn in a wiggly pattern to the bottom of the bowl, trying to fill in as much empty space as possible. The denser you lay down the yarn, the fewer gaps there will be in the finished bowl. Use up the whole piece of yarn.

7 **Repeat steps 4–6 until the bowl is covered.** Cut more strands of yarn and repeat the process, soaking each strand and then laying it onto the bowl. Create a pattern if desired or leave it free-form. Cover the whole bowl without leaving any large gaps.

8 **Place plastic wrap over the yarn.** Add a piece of plastic wrap over the glued yarn. This helps hold the yarn together while it is setting. The plastic does slow the drying process, though, so if you are in a hurry, you could skip this step.

9 **Cover with the other cereal bowl.** Add an identical bowl on top of the plastic wrap (or directly on the yarn). This step helps solidify the shape of the bowl and helps the yarn stick together. You can also skip this step if you're in a rush.

10 **Remove the outside bowl and plastic wrap.** After at least 24 hours, carefully remove the outside bowl and plastic wrap. The plastic wrap may still be stuck if the glue isn't completely dry, so pull it away very carefully. Now give it some more time (about four to six hours) for the outside to fully dry.

11 **Remove the inside bowl.** Once the outside of the bowl is dry, remove the cereal bowl from the inside of the yarn bowl. The plastic wrap should be stuck to the inside of the yarn bowl—leave the plastic wrap on there for now. Allow the yarn bowl to dry for another 24 hours.

12 **Remove the inside plastic wrap.** Carefully pull the plastic wrap away from the yarn once it is completely dry. There still may be some spots that have not fully dried, so take care not to pull the wrap too hard, and wait a little longer before you use the bowl.

OCEAN SCENE

I grew up in Southern California, and going to the beach was a huge part of my childhood. My dad was a surfer, and we had a favorite local beach where we would meet up with friends, play in the waves, watch my dad surf, and relax in the sand. I live far away from the ocean now, but we still try to visit California as much as possible. The beach is my happy place, and I never get tired of it. I wanted to create something that brings my love of the beach to my home. Different shades of blue yarn create a rolling sea, and, just like the waves, no two designs are the same. Even though I have to drive several hundred miles to the ocean now, this art piece brings the beach to my home.

materials + tools

- **Yarn**
  - Medium-weight acrylic or cotton
  - As many shades of blue as desired
  - About 5 yards (4.6 m) (depends on canvas size and number of waves)
- **Canvas or piece of cardboard**
- **Paint**
- **Paintbrush**
- **Pencil**
- **School glue**
- **Scissors**

1 **Paint the canvas.** While the canvas could be left white, a blue background helps make the scene look more like an ocean. You could even use different colors for sand, sky, sea, etc. Paint your canvas as desired, then allow the paint to dry.

2 **Draw ocean waves.** Waves move in many directions, so sketch arcs, curls, and peaks with different starting points. Use a pencil so that the lines can be erased if needed and are easily covered by yarn. Cover as much of the canvas as desired.

3 **Glue on top of the pencil lines.** Apply school glue to one area of the canvas. For this project, you'll work small sections at a time, not all at once. School glue does dry clear, but try to stay on the lines as much as possible.

4 **Glue yarn to the canvas.** You have two methods to choose from here. You can cut yarn ahead of time by laying it over the pencil lines, trimming it to size, and then applying it to the glue. You can also lay the uncut yarn right down on the glue, then trim it to fit. The second method is a little easier, since you can get a more precise size.

5 Continue filling the canvas. Keep working in small sections. Change colors of yarn throughout the piece. You could do each wave in a different color, create an ombre effect, or make each wave a variety of colors, like I've done here.

PETAL
THE WORLD OF
THROUGH AN

PINEAPPLE POM-POMS

When I first started my pom-pom garland business, I wanted to put a spin on traditional pom-poms. I love traditional, solid-colored pom-poms, but I knew that I wanted more variety in my shop. Enter fruit pom-poms! It was summertime, and apparently fruit was on my mind, because I knew I wanted to try to make pom-poms in as many fruit shapes and colors as I could. Through this challenge, these pineapple pom-poms were born. Pineapples don't require much more skill than making a basic pom-pom, but through a little gluing and trimming, the result is truly fun. I originally sold these pineapples in a small size strung on a garland, but they can also be made with a larger pom-pom maker to create a shelf-sitting pineapple. They are darling in any size!

materials + tools

- Yarn
  - Medium-weight acrylic
  - 2 or 3 shades of yellow:
    - For a 3 ½" (9 cm) pom-pom (for shelf-sitting pineapple): about 42 yards (38.4 m)*
  - 1 or 2 shades of green:
    - For a 2" (5 cm) pom-pom (for shelf-sitting pineapple): about 18 yards (16.5 m)*
- **Pom-pom makers in two sizes**
- **Embroidery scissors**
- **Trimming scissors**
- **Hot-glue gun**

*Yarn amounts will vary depending on the weight of yarn and size of pom-pom maker.

1 Hold three shades of yellow yarn. For the pineapple base, three different shades of yarn will be combined to give the pom-pom more texture. This will replicate the rough exterior of a pineapple. If preferred, though, you can use just one shade.

2 Wrap the yellow yarn around the pom-pom maker. Using the larger of the two pom-pom makers, wrap all three pieces of yarn at a time around the whole maker. Complete the pom-pom according to the instructions on page 22, but don't trim it quite yet.

3 Remove the pom-pom from the maker. Once the pom-pom is wound and tied off, remove it from the maker. Large pom-poms tend to be a bit oval shaped when first removed, which is what we want for a pineapple! Fluff the pom-pom to find the oval shape.

4 Roughly trim the pom-pom. Since pineapples have a spiky texture, this pom-pom doesn't need to be trimmed too closely or perfectly. Cut off any extra-long strands and trim so that the oval shape is more visible.

5 Hold two shades of green yarn. Use the smaller of your two pom-pom makers to make the green pineapple top. Just like with the yellow yarn, hold both green yarn strands at the same time when wrapping around the maker.

6 Wrap half of the pom-pom maker. For the top, we are making just half of a pom-pom, not a full pom-pom, so wrap just one side of the pom-pom maker. If you're using cardboard, wrap just half of the cardboard. Cut, tie off, and remove the pom-pom from the maker.

7 Shape the top of the pineapple. Because we have just half of a pom-pom, it will have a side with short yarn and a side with longer yarn. The longer yarn will be the part sticking up out of the pineapple. Shape the half pom-pom with the short yarn on the bottom and the longer yarn on the top.

8 Trim the top of the pineapple. To clean up the top leaves of the pineapple, trim any extra-long ends. The top should still be left longish so that it looks like leaves, but clean up any ends that seem messy.

9 Apply hot glue to the yellow pom-pom. Stand the yellow pom-pom up so that the narrow oval ends are at the top and bottom. Move the yellow yarn on the top out of the way to reveal the center of the pom-pom. Apply a good amount of hot glue to that center.

10 Stick the top to the bottom. Glue the rounded end of the green pom-pom to the yellow pom-pom. Hold the two pieces in place for a minute to allow the hot glue to cool and adhere. If needed, add a little more hot glue around the top to make sure it is secure.

11 Trim around the top of the pineapple. Once the glue has hardened, trim some of the yellow yarn around the base of the green top so that the top is more pronounced. Don't trim too much, though—this is just to help emphasize the separation.

TTLE BOOK OF HYGGE
MEIK WIKING
PETAL
BRING THE OUT
THE MILLIONAIRE MIND
REBECCA
DAPHNE
IN AND OUT OF THE GARDEN
SARA MIDDA
he Secret Lives of Color
Kassia St.Clair
Cold Sassy Tree
Olive Ann Burns
BETWEEN THE WORLD AND ME
& Leaves
ERNEST HEMINGWAY
THE CRYING OF LOT 49
thomas pynchon
1,000 Foods To Eat Before You Die
A Food Lover's Life List
Mimi Sheraton

CHERRY GARLAND

I have loved seeing cherries have their moment to shine recently, since they seem to be popping up on clothing, accessories, household items, and even manicures. We always pack cherries in our bag when we visit the beach in the summer, and we pass them around after soaking up the sun and surf. My kids eat them like candy! This cherry garland brings that summer feeling into your home any time of year. Traditional round pom-poms are used to create the cherries, and they get their signature look from adding yarn stems and felt leaves. While this garland is quite simple to make, you'll end up with darling little cherries that are almost good enough to eat.

materials + tools

- Yarn
  - Medium-weight acrylic yarn
  - Pink or red for cherries:
    - For a 1" (2.5 cm) pom-pom: about 8 yards (7.3 m) per pom-pom*
  - Brown for cherry stems:
    - About 3" (7.5 cm) per cherry
  - Green for garland string:
    - About 3–5 yards (2.7–4.6 m)
- **Small or medium pom-pom maker (or both)**
- **Embroidery scissors**
- **Trimming scissors**
- **Plastic or metal yarn needle with large eye**
- **Green felt**
- **Leaf template on page 162**
- **Green pen or water-soluble fabric pen**
- **Hot-glue gun**

*Yarn amounts will vary depending on the weight of yarn and size of pom-pom maker.

1 **Make two pom-poms.** Using a small pom-pom maker, make two pom-poms using the basic instructions on page 22. Any pink or red color of yarn works well for cherries. Trim the pom-poms so that they are roughly the same size.

2 **Cut two stems of yarn.** With the brown yarn, cut two pieces that measure about 2"–3" (5–7.5 cm) long. These can always be trimmed down later. Tie a knot toward the bottom of each stem.

3 **Add the stems to the cherries.** String a plastic or metal yarn needle with a brown-yarn stem. In one cherry pom-pom, try to find the center string that was used for tying the pom-pom, and insert the needle through it. This will keep the knot on the brown yarn from going all the way through the pom-pom.

4 **Pull the stem into the cherry.** While holding the pom-pom carefully, pull the brown yarn through all the way to the knot. Stop pulling when the stem has reached the knot. Don't pull too hard or the yarn may go all the way through.

5 Create the felt leaves. Using the leaf template on page 162, trace two sets of leaves onto green felt. Use a green pen to make the marks less visible, or hide the pen marks when gluing in steps 6–7. Cut both sets of leaves out of the felt.

6 Hot-glue the stems to one leaf. Apply a dab of hot glue to the center of one leaf set. Stick both brown stems to the hot glue. If any pen marks are visible on the felt, make sure that's the side facing up and getting glued, since it will get covered by the second set of leaves.

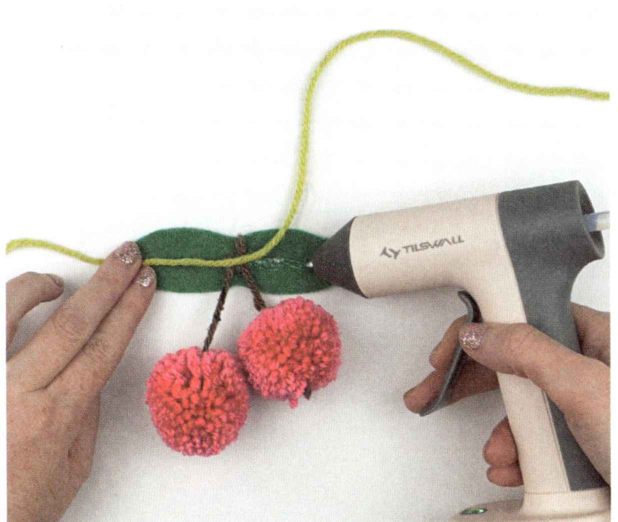

7 Start stringing the garland. Cut a long piece of green yarn to the desired length of the garland. Spread a line of hot glue horizontally about a third of the way or halfway down from the top of the leaves. Working quickly, stick the green yarn to the line of hot glue.

8 Add the top set of leaves. Immediately spread hot glue all around the edge of the first set of leaves, then place the second set of leaves on top, matching the edges up and sandwiching the garland string between them. Repeat all steps to continue adding cherries to the garland, spacing them evenly along the string.

WATERMELON GARLAND

In keeping with our pom-pom fruit theme, I had to add one more of my favorite fruit pom-poms: watermelons! As I mentioned in the beginning of the book, I used to make and sell fruit garlands in my Etsy shop. I started with strawberries, which then led to watermelons, which then led to pineapples and various other fruits. The watermelon garlands were always a hit, and they were one of my favorites too! Like the cherry garland, this garland is also made from traditional, round pom-poms, but two colors of yarn are wound around the maker to give the appearance of the inside and outside of a watermelon. Once you create all your fruit pom-poms from this book, you'll be able to make a whole fruit salad!

materials + tools

- **Yarn**
  - Medium-weight acrylic yarn
  - Pink and black for watermelon interiors:
    - For a 2" (5 cm) pom-pom: about 18 yards (16.5 m) per pom-pom*
  - Dark green and medium green for watermelon exteriors:
    - For a 2" (5 cm) pom-pom: about 9 yards (8.2 m) per color per pom-pom*
  - Multicolor black and white for garland string:
    - About 3–5 yards (2.7–4.6 m)
- **Small or medium pom-pom maker (or both)**
- **Embroidery scissors**
- **Trimming scissors**
- **Plastic or metal yarn needle with large eye**

*Yarn amounts will vary depending on the weight of yarn and size of pom-pom maker.

1 Start one pink pom-pom. To make a watermelon interior, use a medium pom-pom maker and begin winding pink yarn like usual. After the pink has gone around a few times, wrap black yarn a few times around the maker. This creates the seeds.

2 Wrap the whole pom-pom maker. Continue alternating more pink, then a few winds of black on both sides of the pom-pom maker. The more black you use, the more seeds there will be. Spread out the black yarn to create a scattered appearance.

3 Trim the pom-pom. Finish the pom-pom and remove it from the maker. When removed from the maker, the black seeds will finally be visible. These watermelons should be round, so trim them closely.

4 Make several pink pom-poms. To add more variety to the garland, use two different shades of pink when making your collection of watermelon interiors. The garland will alternate between the pink (interior) melons and the green (rind) melons.

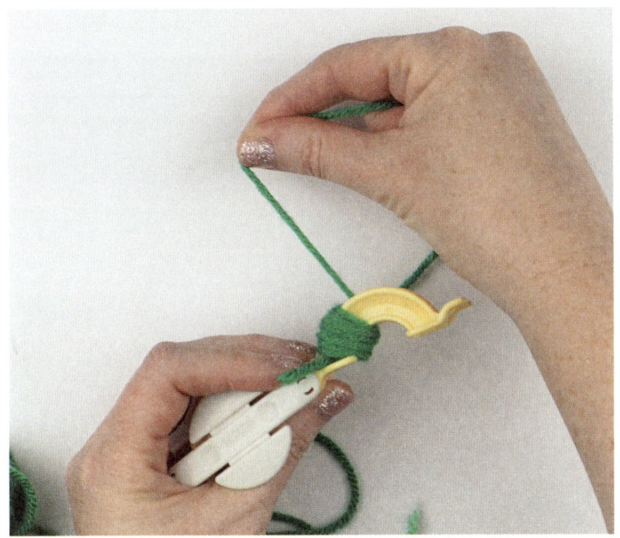

5 Start one green pom-pom. The watermelon rind pom-poms will have a striped appearance. Choose two colors of green yarn. Begin with one green, wrapping it over and over in the same spot on the pom-pom maker. Fill that spot all the way with that green.

6 Make stripes in the green pom-pom. Use the second green to wrap a full section right next to the first section of the first green. Fill this second section all the way to the max. This is how you create stripes on a pom-pom.

7 Finish both sides of the green pom-pom. Follow this pattern of alternating green colors by wrapping in full sections right next to each other. Fill one whole side of the maker, then do the same thing on the other side. Tie up and remove the pom-pom from the maker. Trim to make it round. Make a collection of these watermelon rind pom-poms.

8 String into a garland. Use yarn, string, or baker's twine for your garland string. Thread a metal yarn needle with your garland string and insert the needle into the center of the first pom-pom. Hold the pom-pom carefully and pull the string through. Alternate pink and green pom-poms all the way along.

BOW GARLAND

I have always loved bows. As a little girl in the '80s and '90s, I wore my share of bows in my hair. More recently, bows have made a major comeback, and they can be found on everything from T-shirts to Christmas trees. I am here for all of it! I love an excuse to add an extra bow. I have made another variation of a yarn-bow garland before, but I used thin yarn and stitched the bows onto a string. I loved that garland, but it was a little tricky to feed the thin yarn onto the needle. In this upgraded version, I used bulky, super-bulky, and jumbo yarn to make the bows the star of the show. This project works best if you use yarn that is all similar in weight—I tried mixing in a slightly smaller yarn, and it didn't hold up well against the larger weights. There's no stitching required for the assembly of this garland either—you simply tie the bows to one another! By changing up the colors of yarn, this garland can be made for different holidays or seasons, or you can make it in neutral colors and leave it up all year round.

materials + tools

- **Yarn**
  - Bulky, super-bulky, or jumbo weight (keep the weights similar)
  - As many colors and textures as desired
  - About 25" (63 cm) per bow
- **Scissors**

BOW GARLAND

1 Make two loops with the yarn. With a 25" (63 cm) piece of yarn, make two loops that are evenly sized and spaced. If you want longer bow tails, cut the yarn longer. Bulkier yarn may require a little more length too, since it takes more yarn to make a bow.

2 Cross the two loops. Put one loop in front of the other, but make sure to keep a circle in the middle. I use my fingers to keep that space visible, since it often gets covered by the bulky yarn.

3 Wrap the loops around. Like tying a shoelace, wrap one loop around the other and insert it into the space that was made when crossing the loops. Bulkier yarn is a little trickier to work with, so leave that space large enough for the bulky loop.

4 Pull both loops to make a bow. Tighten both loops and even them out to make them about the same size. If the bow tails are too long, trim them to make them even. Each bow needs to be tied tightly so that the garland holds together.

5 Insert another piece of yarn into the existing bow. Choose and cut your next piece of yarn. Feed it through one loop of the first finished bow.

6 Make two loops with the new yarn. Like the first bow, begin by making two loops. For this bow, include the loop of the first bow within one loop of the new bow you're making. Each bow on the garland will be attached to the loop of the bow next to it.

7 Cross the loops of the new bow. Just as in step 2, cross the two loops over one another. Keep the space open below the two loops. Wrap one loop around the other and pull it through the space like before.

8 Tighten the bow. Pull the loops to tighten them, then even them out. Trim the tails if needed. Continue adding bows by repeating steps 6–7 until the garland has reached the desired length. Hang the garland on a mantel, bookcase, or wall to bring a little extra sweetness to any room.

WRAPPED WIRE SHAPES

materials + tools

- Yarn
  - Light, medium, or bulky weight
  - At least 1 color, but as many as desired
  - About 8 yards (7.3 m) per shape (depends on size of shape)
- **Wire (thick but pliable)**
- **Pipe cleaners (optional alternative to wire)**
- **Wire cutters**
- **Scissors**
- **Pliers**
- **Hot-glue gun**
- **Embroidery floss**
- **Sequins**
- **School glue**
- **Cardboard**

Inspiration for art projects can come from anywhere. I was shopping in a clothing store when I came across some hanging ornaments that were being used as part of the store's décor. The ornaments were wire shapes wrapped in thread and embellished with sequins and buttons. While I wasn't expecting to find wire ornaments in a clothing store, I was instantly attracted to them and knew that they were something I could try to re-create and make my own. I pulled out some thick wire that I had at home and, of course, swapped out the thread for yarn. I embellished my wire shapes with sequins that I already had in my craft stash, giving the project my own personal touch. I also created another variation to this project by using a piece of cardboard that is wrapped with yarn. I like to think of this project as a good "stash buster" because you can use materials you already have. The completed results are a fun addition to any space!

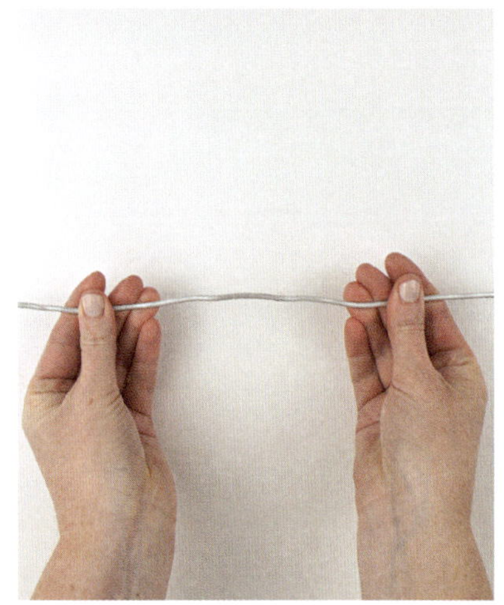

1 Cut a length of wire. Before the wire is cut, roughly bend it into a shape to see how much wire you'll need. Your shape could be a heart, a moon, a star, etc. Using wire cutters, cut the wire to the desired length. Then bend the cut wire into a straight line, being careful with the sharp edges.

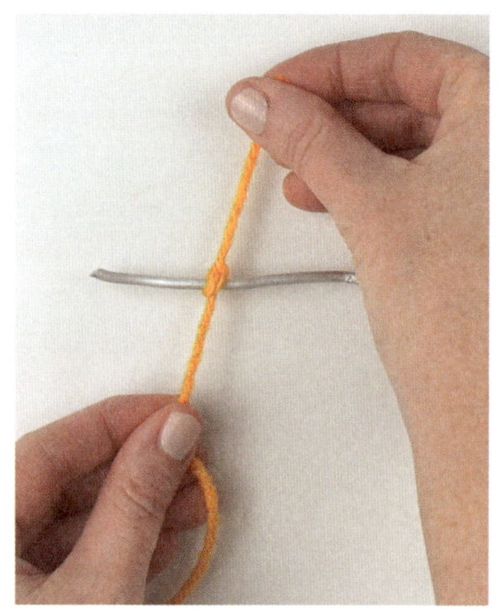

2 Tie the yarn onto the wire. Choose a color of yarn and tie it in a knot close to one end of the wire. While the wire can be shaped prior to adding yarn, it is a little easier to wrap when it is in a line rather than already in a closed shape.

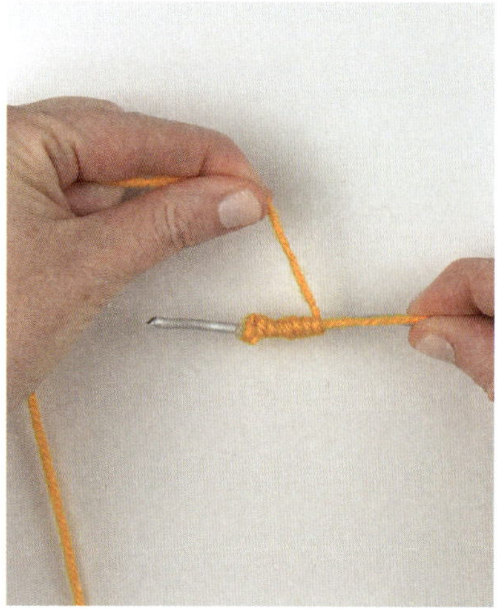

3 Wrap the yarn around the wire. Start by wrapping the yarn over its own knot to cover it. Continue wrapping along the wire with that yarn color for as long as desired. At the end of the color, knot the yarn around the wire again.

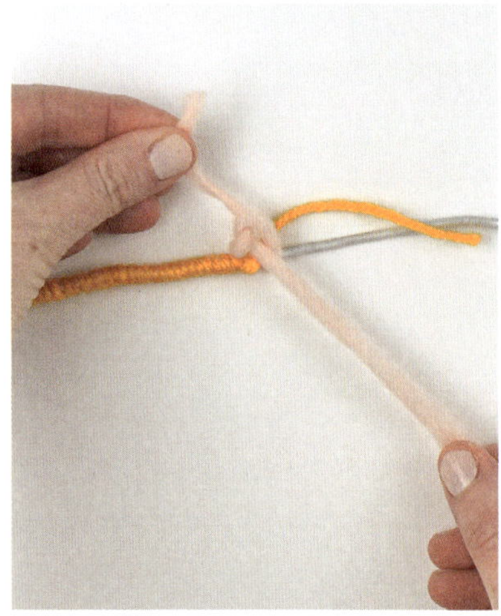

4 Add a second yarn color. Tie a new color of yarn to the wire like in step 2. Tie the knot over the end of the previous yarn so that the first yarn end and the new yarn end will get covered as you begin to wrap with the new color.

5 Wrap the yarn around the wire. Like in step 3, wrap the new color of yarn around the wire, covering the end of both the first yarn and the new yarn. Repeat this pattern of adding and wrapping yarn until you are almost at the end of your wire.

6 Connect the two wire ends. The ends of the wire were left bare so that they are easier to twist together now. Wrap one end around the other, using pliers, until the join is securely fastened. Take care with the sharp wire edges.

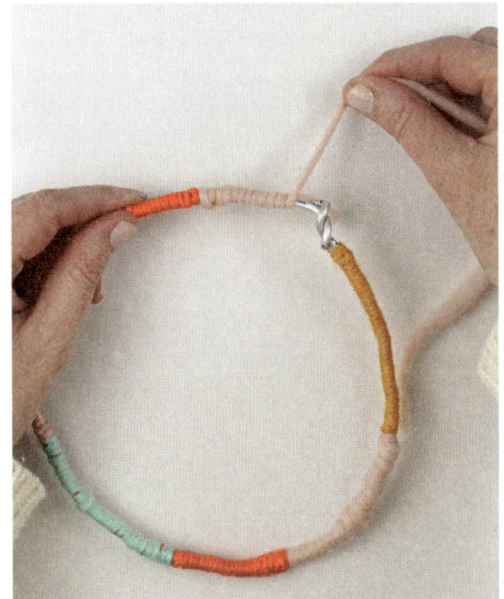

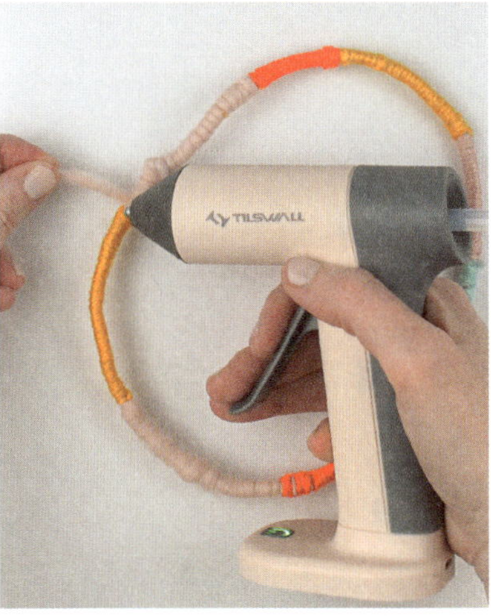

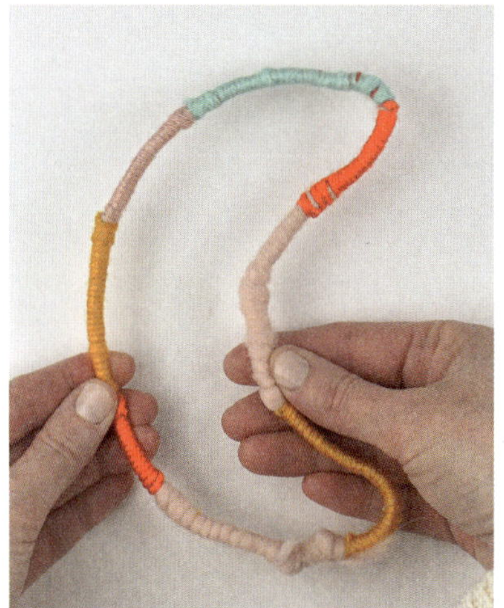

7 **Wrap yarn over the wire ends.** Either using a new piece of yarn or continuing with a piece that is still on the wire, wrap the yarn around the wire join. Make sure the entire wire is covered. The yarn will be a little bulky at the join, but it won't be very noticeable once embellishments are added.

8 **Secure the end of the yarn.** Tie a knot around the wire with the last color of yarn. Since the end of this yarn can't be hidden under more wrapping, use a dot of hot glue to secure the end to the yarn and wire. Trim any excess yarn.

9 **Bend the wire into shape.** To make most basic shapes, your hands will work well for bending the wire. For more-detailed shapes, you may need pliers. Try to make the wire as smooth as possible, without many bumps.

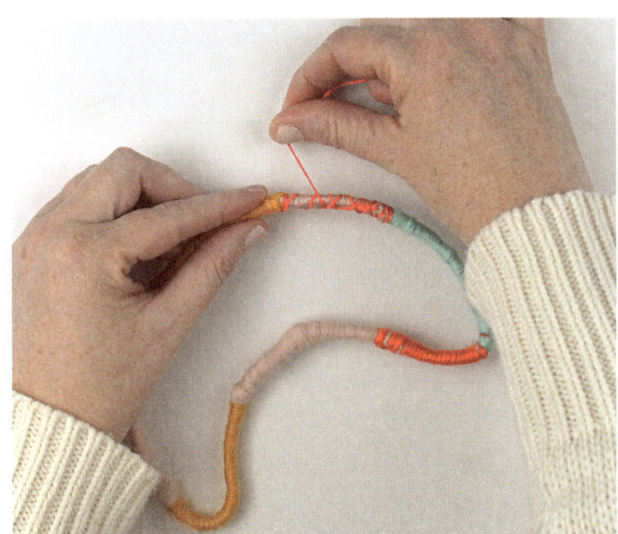

10 **Add embroidery floss embellishments.** For extra dimension and detail, wrap a piece of embroidery floss around a section of the yarn and wire. Tie it on like the yarn and hot-glue the ends in place. Zigzag or spiral the floss around the yarn to make designs.

11 **Glue sequins to the shape.** Glue sequins, 1 rhinestone, buttons, glitter, etc. to the shape using school glue. For heavier items like buttons, hot glue may be needed. Add as many or as few embellishments as desired.

Pipe-Cleaner Variation

1 **Twist two pipe cleaners together.** Since pipe cleaners are not very long, two pipe cleaners will probably need to be twisted together to make one long wire. Excess pipe cleaner can be cut off later.

2 **Decorate and shape the pipe cleaners.** Follow steps 2–11 to create a wire shape using your pipe-cleaner wire. Make sure to cover the entire pipe-cleaner shape so that the pipe-cleaner texture is not showing under the yarn. Cut any extra pipe cleaner before rejoining the ends.

Cardboard Variation

1 **Wrap yarn around a cardboard shape.** Cut a shape out of a cardboard box. Hold one end of a piece of yarn against the center of the shape and begin wrapping the yarn around the shape. Cover the yarn end so that gets held in place. You could also tape the yarn down to the cardboard.

2 **Cover the whole shape with yarn.** Wrap around and around, trying to cover the entire surface of the cardboard. To change colors, the end of one strand of yarn can be tied to another color, then wrapped as usual. The star points will be impossible to cover entirely, but get as close to the points as you can.

3 **Tie a knot with the final piece of yarn.** Insert the yarn end under a piece of wrapped yarn on the back of the shape for added security, then tie the end into a knot. Trim any long ends. Secure the end with hot glue if necessary.

4 **Add embellishments.** This cardboard shape can also be decorated like the wire shapes by adding sequins or glitter. I kept mine simple without embellishments, but these are cute either way!

materials + tools

- Yarn
  - Any weight or texture
  - At least 1 color, but as many as desired
  - 20"–25" (51–63 cm) per length of yarn (depends on yarn weight and dowel size)
- Wooden dowel
- Scissors
- Pom-poms or tassels (optional)

HANGING FLAG

One of the things I love about yarn is how much variety there is. Yarn can be found in every color of the rainbow, so projects can be designed exactly to your liking. Yarn also comes in many textures and weights, making it the perfect material for hundreds of projects. This hanging flag is a great way to show off all those fun yarn colors and textures, and it couldn't be easier to make! I simply used a set of colors that I liked for my flag, but these can also be made in colors for different countries or for various holidays. It is also a fun way to experiment with different tying techniques. To add variety to my flag, I tried out different knots and braids, and I added pom-poms and tassels. Anything goes with these flags, and they make wonderful wall art!

1 Loop a piece of yarn behind the dowel. Cut the yarn into long lengths, since it will be doubled up. It is better to cut longer pieces of yarn than shorter ones, since it is easy to trim off excess at the end. Fold the yarn in half and lay the loop under the dowel.

2 Fold the loop over the dowel. Fold the loop down over the front of the dowel, then pull the tails up through the loop. Don't place the loop too close to the edge of the dowel, since it may slide off.

3 Tighten to secure. Secure the yarn to the dowel by pulling the ends tightly. This should be enough to keep the yarn in place, but if you want extra hold, you can double-knot the yarn after tightening the loop. Add yarn by using this basic technique as many times as you want.

4 Create braided sections. To create braided sections, add multiple strands of yarn like normal, then divide the strands into three. Begin braiding the yarn by moving each outer section to the center. Use as many strands as desired to increase or decrease the braid's thickness. Tie a knot at the bottom of the braid.

5 Create knotted sections. For a loopy knotted section, separate several strands of yarn into three sections. Take an outside and center section and tie a knot a few inches down from the top. Then take the center and other outside section and tie another knot a few inches down from the first. Repeat to the bottom.

6 Add bows. In one or two spots, gather up some strands of yarn and tie a bow onto the section, using a separate piece of yarn. Add these anywhere more detail is desired. Pom-poms and tassels can also be added at this point.

7 Trim the ends. To make the ends even, trim them with sharp scissors. A large ruler or piece of cardboard can be laid on top of the yarn and used as a guide to help keep the ends even.

8 Add a piece of yarn for hanging. Knot a piece of yarn onto one end of the dowel. Knot the other end of the yarn to the other end of the dowel. Use this piece of yarn for hanging the flag from a wall, window, or door.

WOVEN STRAW CHAIN

materials + tools

- Yarn
  - Medium-weight acrylic or cotton
  - At least 1 color, but as many as desired
  - About 12 yards (11 m) per chain link
- **Three plastic straws**
- **Scissors**
- **Washi tape or masking tape**
- **Hot-glue gun (optional)**

I remember making paper chains when I was younger to help count down the days until Christmas or the days until summer vacation. While it was always so rewarding to tear off a chain each day, knowing that I was one day closer to something amazing, I also loved the look of that cute chain hanging from my wall. This woven yarn chain is a project that uses an unlikely kitchen item to create the weaving: drinking straws! When the straws are taped together, they create a sort of loom where yarn can be wrapped over and under each straw. The result is a colorful miniature yarn weaving. While I turned these weavings into a chain, they can also be made into friendship bracelets or even bookmarks.

1 Cut three pieces of yarn. Cut three pieces of yarn that are about double the length of the straws. If the straws have a bendable part, cut off the entire bendable part (including the extendable section), leaving just the large, straight part of the straw. If the straws don't have a bend, they can be cut to any length. These straws are about 7" (18 cm) long.

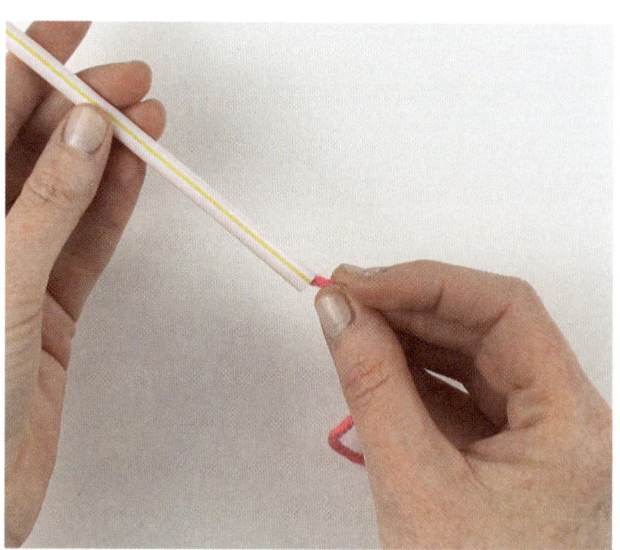

2 Insert the yarn into the straws. Feed each piece of yarn into a straw. Leave about 1" (2.5 cm) of yarn sticking out of the top of the straw, with the remaining yarn trailing out of the bottom of the straw.

3 Knot the strands of yarn. Take all three of the short sections of yarn at the top of each straw and tie them together into a knot. Do this on a flat surface so that the straws don't slip off the yarn. If a straw does fall off, feed it back on.

4 Tape the straws together. Use a piece of washi or masking tape to tape all the way around the three straws at the top. Keep the straws flat and in a row. Try to capture the yarn knot inside the tape too, so that the yarn stays put.

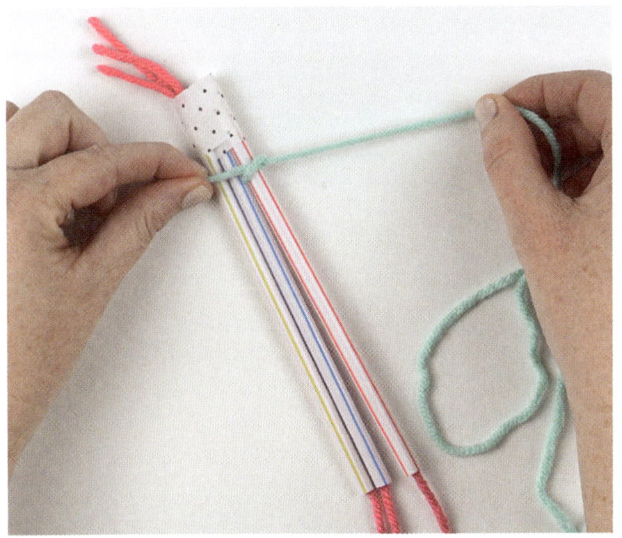

5 **Tie a strand of yarn onto a straw.** Take a new piece of yarn and tie it onto any straw just below the tape with a double knot. Keep the end of the yarn long for now, since it can be trimmed and secured with hot glue later.

6 **Weave the yarn around the straws.** Wrap the yarn around the bottom of the straw next to the knot, then wrap it around the top of the next straw. Like any weaving project, this pattern will be repeated in an over-under manner throughout.

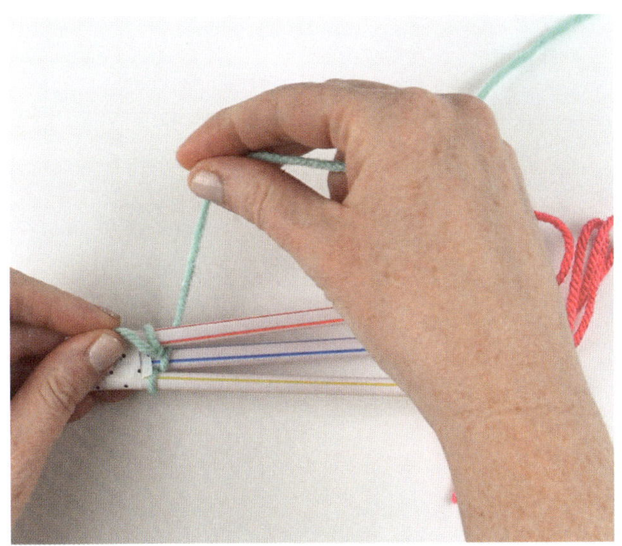

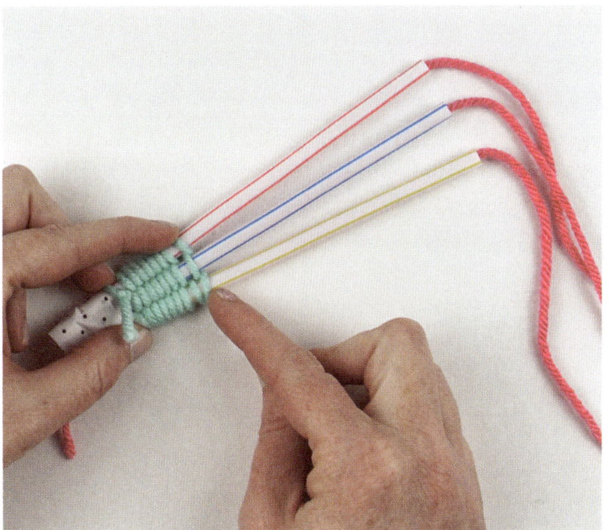

7 **Weave the next row.** For the second row, wrap the yarn around each straw in the opposite direction from the first row. When you finish the second row, each straw should have one full visible loop of yarn around it.

8 **Continue weaving.** Repeat the over-under pattern until you are done with the color. Loop the yarn around a straw and insert the end into the loop to knot the yarn. These ends can be covered by the next color of yarn or hot-glued when finished, to eliminate loose ends.

9 **Add another color of yarn.** Like in step 5, tie a new strand of yarn onto a straw. Weave it until you're done with the color. Repeat, weaving and adding new colors, until the straws are almost completely covered. Knot the final color onto a straw.

10 **Remove the tape.** Carefully remove the tape from the top of the straws. Hold the knot at the top while removing the tape so that the tape doesn't pull the three strands of yarn out of the straws.

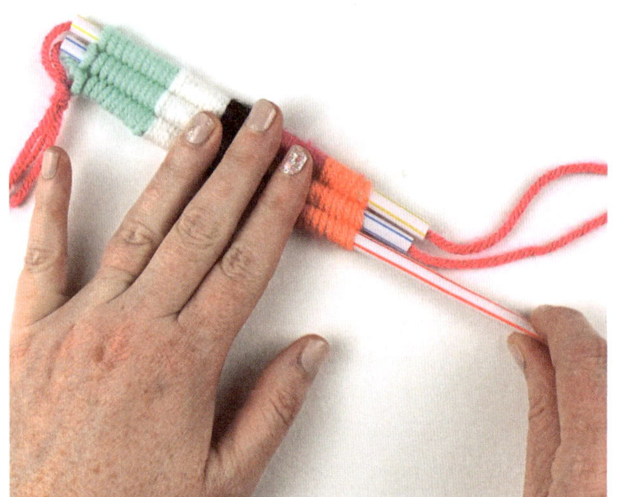

11 **Remove the straws.** Hold on to the weaving firmly and push and pull each straw out of the weaving. It may take a little wiggling to get the straws free. The first straw is always the trickiest. Make sure the three strands of yarn stay put inside the weaving—the weaving will fall apart if those three strands are removed.

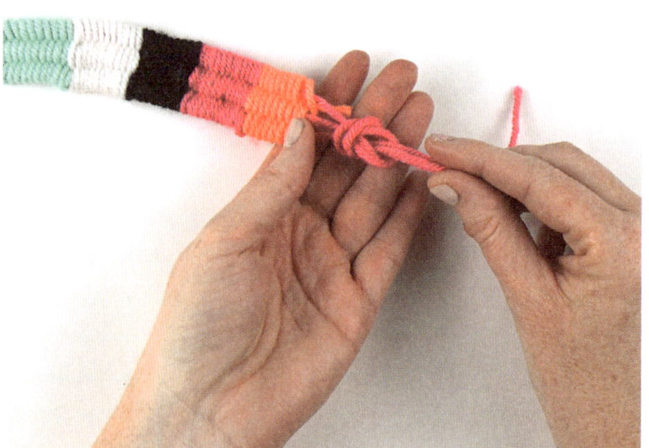

12 **Knot the strands at the bottom.** Like in step 3, make a knot with the three strands of yarn at the bottom of the weaving. This finally secures the weaving on the three strands of yarn.

13 **Tie the ends together.** Tie the two ends of the yarn together in a double knot. If you're making a bracelet, the weaving can be tied onto a wrist at this point. Trim any long yarn ends with scissors.

14 **Repeat in a chain.** Repeat steps 1–12 to make another weaving. Before tying the two ends together, though, insert the second weaving into the first chain link and then tie it together. Repeat until the chain reaches the desired length.

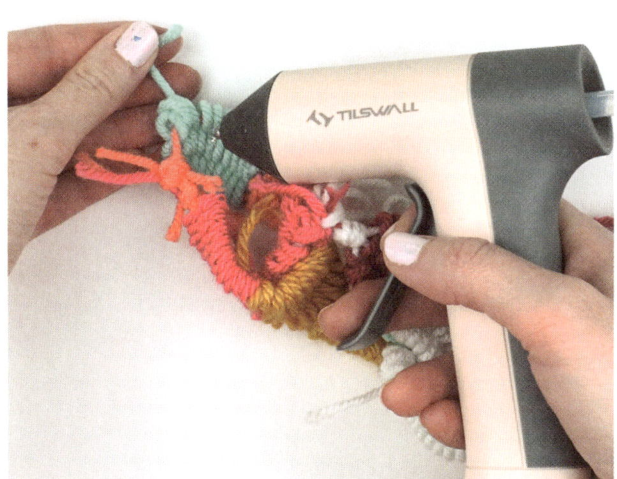

15 **Hot-glue the yarn ends to the chain.** To make the chain look tidier, the ends of the woven colors of yarn can be hot-glued to the insides of the chains. This step can be skipped if you prefer a messier look.

tip

Make sure the three strings don't come out of the straws or the weaving as you work. The weaving can unravel without those strings running through them.

TIED WREATH

materials + tools

- Yarn
  - Bulky to super-bulky weight for the base of the wreath, 1 color:
    - For a 12" (31 cm) wreath: about 30 yards (27.4 m)
  - Light to bulky weight for the colored pieces, at least 1 color, but as many as desired:
    - For a 12" (31 cm) wreath: about 15 yards (13.7 m)
- Ruler or measuring tape
- Scissors
- Wire wreath frame in any size
- Fabric-stiffener spray (optional)

A few years ago, my sister sent me a picture of an expensive wreath that she had spotted in an upscale store. The wreath was made of chunky yarn in various colors, and it looked like it was almost looped onto a wreath form. Knowing that I love yarn and also love a challenge to re-create expensive home décor, she sent me the photo, asking if I could make a wreath like it. It was a darling wreath, so I knew I had to try to make one and put my own spin on it. Instead of looping yarn like the original, I bought a wire wreath frame and tied small pieces of yarn onto the wire. After filling the wreath with a solid color, I went back and added smaller pieces of colored yarn. I loved the result! This wreath looks like it could be purchased in a boutique, but it is very inexpensive to make!

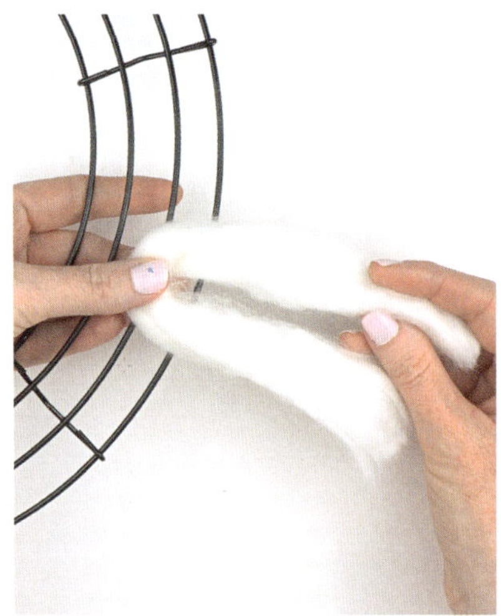

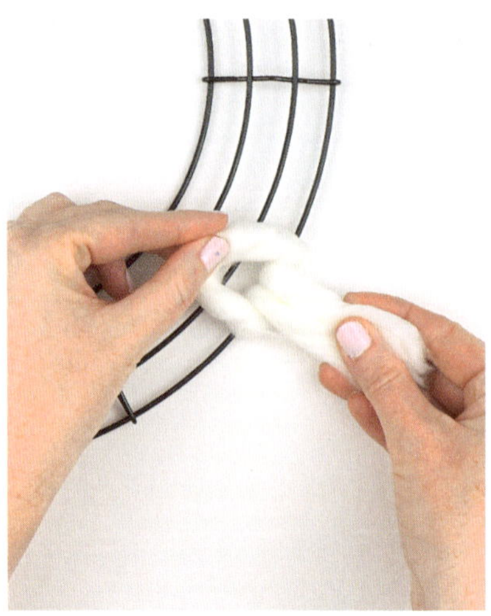

1 **Cut pieces of yarn.** Using the bulky or super-bulky base color of yarn, cut many pieces of yarn into about 9" (23 cm) lengths. It's easier to cut a lot of pieces now, then cut more later if needed. If your yarn is thinner, it may not need to be as long, since the knot will be smaller.

2 **Lay the yarn piece on the wreath.** Set the wreath frame so that the outside edge is flat on the table. Take one piece of yarn and fold it in half to make a loop. Lay the loop on the top of the frame over the outer edge. The yarn will be tied starting on the outside layer, then moving into the center.

3 **Tie the yarn onto the wreath.** Take the ends of the yarn and wrap them around the outside wire. Feed them back through the inside of the frame and through the yarn loop. Pull the ends to tighten and make a knot around the wire.

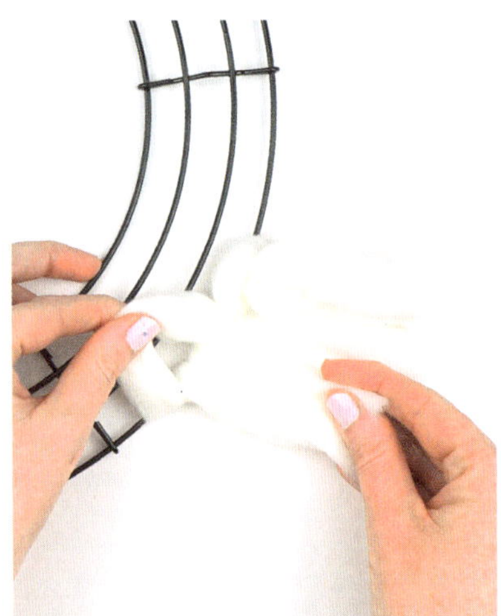

4 **Continue tying yarn around the outside.** Just like before, add another piece of the base-layer yarn. Make sure to pull the ends tightly so that the knot is tight and doesn't come undone.

5 **Add colorful yarn to the edge.** This step can be done after the entire base layer is filled or during the process of filling the base layer. Take smaller, colorful pieces of yarn and tie them onto the wreath just like the bulkier base yarn.

6 **Begin the next round of yarn.** If the wreath has four wire circles like this one, skip the next circle and work on the one after that. In my wreath form, the wire circle directly after the outer edge goes upward, which would make the yarn poke out oddly, so it makes sense to skip it.

7 Tie yarn onto the second round. Just like for the outside edge, begin tying yarn onto your target circle. Pull each piece tightly. Add colorful yarn either as you go or after the round is complete.

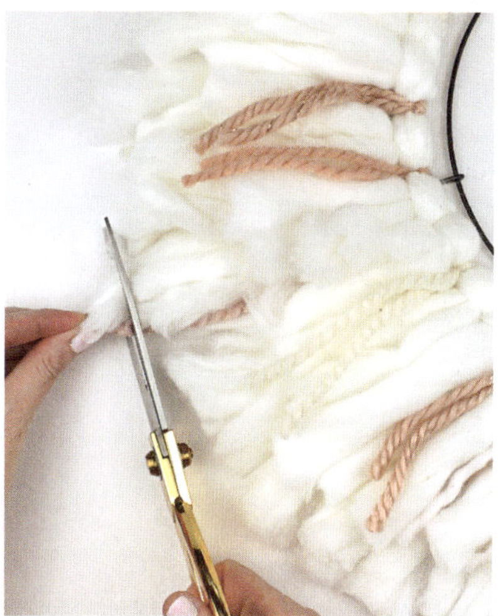

8 Trim the outside yarn. The outside yarn will be the longest layer of yarn, so don't trim it too much. Trim only to even out the yarn ends. It does not need to be perfect—just cut any long pieces that stand out.

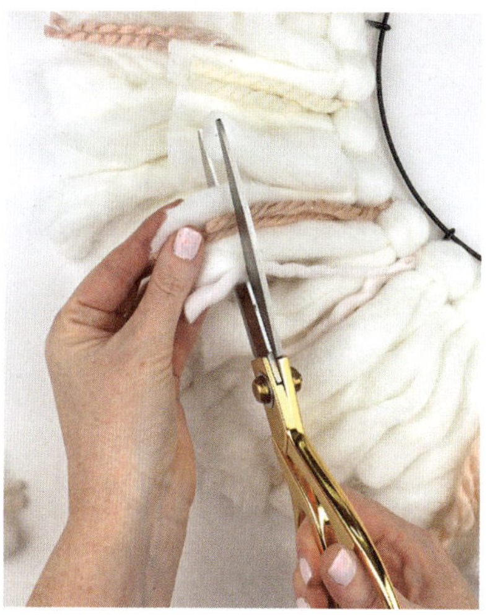

9 Trim the second round of yarn. This round should be shorter than the outside round. Trim any extra-long pieces and also trim everything down so that the outside layer is clearly exposed. Again, it doesn't need to be perfect.

10 Tie yarn onto the inner round. For the final round, tie yarn onto the innermost wire circle. This round is the trickiest to feed the yarn into, since the knots from the previous round are a little bit in the way. Knot the yarn onto the round like in other rounds, adding colorful yarn as desired.

11 Trim the inside round of yarn. The inside round should be the shortest of all the rounds. Trim the yarn down so that the second round can be clearly seen under it. Examine the entire wreath and make sure that it is circular and doesn't have any long strands.

12 Add fabric stiffener. This step is optional. Since gravity does want to pull the yarn down over time, fabric stiffener can help your wreath hold its shape. Protect your workspace, then spray fabric stiffener all over the yarn and allow to dry completely.

materials + tools

- Yarn
  - Light to bulky weight
  - 1 color
  - For a 10" (25 cm) hoop: about 6 yards (5.5 m)
- Macramé ring or embroidery hoop
- Cheesecloth, fabric, or yarn for wrapping around the ring
- Scissors
- Hot-glue gun
- Yarn and ribbon of various weights for the tail strings, cut into about 24" (61 cm) lengths
- Pom-poms, tassels, bows, etc. for embellishment (optional)

SPIDERWEBS

How could I write a book about yarn crafts and not include a spiderweb project? For this project, spiderwebs are created using a round weaving technique. Warp strings (the base, vertical strings on a loom) are strung onto a ring, then yarn is wrapped around those warp strings to make a spiderweb design. Once you master setting up the round "loom," you can make other projects by weaving over and under warp strings in the same way. By adding more yarn and by weaving rather than wrapping, you can create entirely different woven projects. I added yarn and ribbon tails to my spiderweb, since I wanted mine to be cute and not too creepy!

1 Hot-glue the cheesecloth, fabric, or yarn to the ring. Macramé rings are smooth and slick, so adding a layer of texture helps the warp strings to stay in place. Cheesecloth is a fun addition for Halloween, since it looks ghostly. Put a dot of hot glue on the ring, then stick the cheesecloth to it.

2 Wrap the cheesecloth around the ring. Begin wrapping the cloth all the way around the ring. Every few inches or so, add another dot of hot glue so that the cloth doesn't slide around. Continue wrapping to the end.

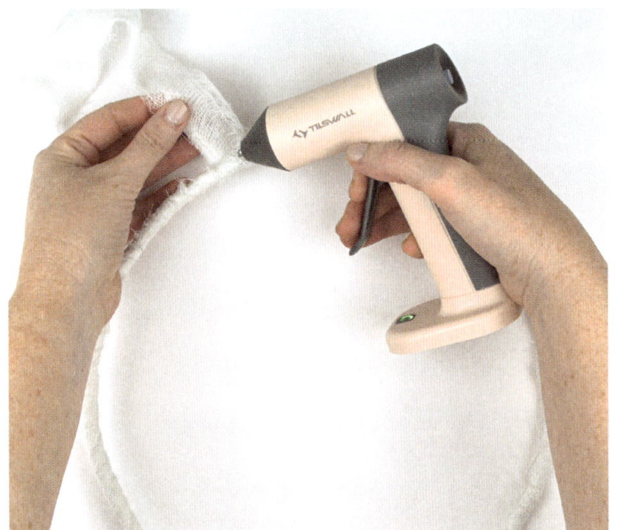

3 Hot-glue the cloth to the ring. Once the whole ring is covered, apply a final dot of hot glue to the end of the ring to secure the cheesecloth. Trim any excess cloth. Make sure the whole ring is covered before you continue.

4 Tie a warp string onto the ring. Tie the end of a piece of light to bulky yarn (I'm using medium) onto the ring. Double-knot it. This will be the warp that our spiderweb design will be tied onto. (In weaving terms, the warp yarns run vertically and are pulled tight.)

5 **Zigzag the yarn around the ring.** Begin creating a zigzag pattern with the yarn. The more lines you make across, the more warp strings the design will have. Each point on the edge will be one warp string. Go all the way around the ring in this pattern.

6 **Tie the end of the yarn onto the ring.** Once the ring is filled with the desired number of warp strings, knot the end of the yarn back at the same place as the beginning knot. It is best if the yarn starts and ends at the same point on the ring.

7 **Cinch the strings at the center.** To make the warp strings line up on top of each other, the center needs to be cinched together. This will help the web have a distinct center and distinct lines. Insert a piece of yarn inside any section, making sure to hold the end.

8 **Gather the center.** Use the center string to go back and forth over the warp strings on the ring. Continue to hold on to the end of the center string. Tighten the string as it is woven over and under the warp strings.

9 Tie a knot in the center. Once all the warp strings have been gathered by the center string, pull it tightly and make a knot in the center. All the warp strings should be lined up on top of each other now. Trim the long ends of the center string.

10 Tie a new piece of yarn onto a warp string. To begin the rounds of the web, double-knot a piece of yarn onto one warp string. Place this knot toward the outside edge of the ring, since this will be the outermost layer on the web.

11 Wrap the yarn around the next warp string. Stretch the yarn to the next warp string on the ring. Wind the yarn once around the warp string so that it is secure. No knotting is necessary, since the yarn will hold in place. Continue wrapping around each warp string on the ring.

12 Knot the yarn at the end. Once the yarn has been wrapped around each string and is back to where it started, double-knot the yarn again onto the first string. Make this second knot close to the first knot to close the circle neatly. Trim any long ends.

13 Weave more rounds. Repeat steps 10–12 to continue to add more rounds to the spiderweb. The more rounds you add, the more detail the web will have. Keep all knots on the backside of the web.

14 Add fringe to the bottom. If desired, add embellishment to the bottom of the web. Anything can be used to add fringe, including yarn, tulle, ribbon, fabric, etc. Either knot the pieces to the bottom or double up the fringe and loop it around the ring.

15 Add pom-poms to the fringe. For added detail and charm, string a few pom-poms onto the fringe. Choose a medium-weight piece of yarn to tie onto the ring. Thread the end of the yarn through a needle, then insert the needle into the center of a pom-pom. Remove the needle, then knot the end of the yarn.

16 Trim the fringe. To even out the fringe at the bottom, trim across with sharp scissors. If you added pom-poms to the fringe, take care not to cut off the pom-poms. Add plastic or pom-pom spiders to the web to make it spookier.

SPIDERS

My kids love Halloween. Two of my kids would even say that Halloween is their favorite holiday! While I'm a fan of cute costumes, candy, and carving pumpkins, I'm not a big fan of scary Halloween décor. Ever since my kids were little, we have put large, fake spiders on the outside of our house. Last year, we even upped the game by adding large, fake spiderwebs and smaller spiders in addition to our larger spiders. That is about as scary and creepy as I like to get! Pom-pom spiders are the perfect Halloween decorations because they are more cute than scary. They are also the perfect follow-up craft to our woven spiderwebs. Once you have crafted a cute web, you need a cute spider to go with it! Secure these pom-pom spiders to your web and enjoy a creepy-cute holiday!

materials + tools

- **Yarn**
  - Light, medium, or bulky weight in 1–3 different weights/textures
  - Black
  - For a 3" (7.5 cm) pom-pom: about 42 yards (38.4 m)
  - For a 2" (5 cm) pom-pom: about 18 yards (16.5 m)
- **Pom-pom maker**
- **Embroidery scissors**
- **Trimming scissors**
- **Pipe cleaners**
- **Hot-glue gun**
- **Googly eyes, beads, or buttons**

1 **Hold several pieces of black yarn together.** To make this pom-pom, use several strands of black yarn at the same time. Using several strands will make the pom-pom process quicker and will distribute the different yarns evenly around the maker.

2 **Wrap the pom-pom maker.** Follow the basic instructions on page 22 to wind the three strands of yarn around the maker. A plastic maker or cardboard maker can be used. Any size of maker works. Wind, tie, and remove the pom-pom from the maker.

3 **Trim the pom-pom.** To make the spider appear hairier, leave the pom-pom a little shaggy. If you're using eyelash yarn as shown, it will help give a hairy appearance. Trim as much as desired to make the pom-pom mostly round and even.

4 **Cut pipe-cleaner legs.** The spider's legs can be any length. Using sharp scissors, cut pipe cleaners to create the desired number of legs (eight legs is optional here—it's your spider!). The legs should be about the same length so that the spider sits evenly.

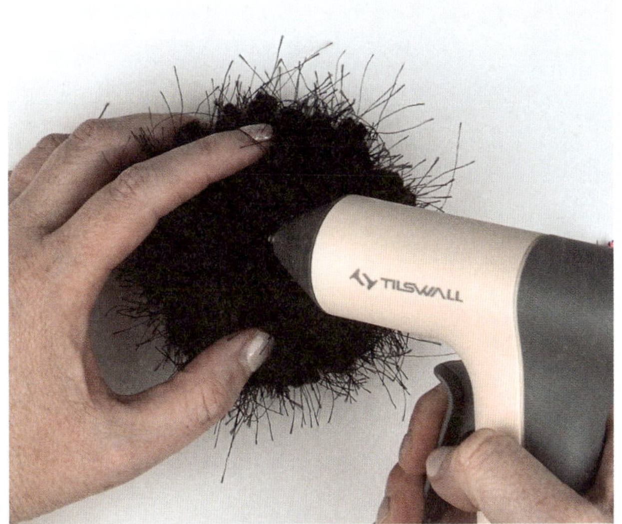

5 Apply hot glue to the center of the pom-pom. Move some of the yarn strands out of the way to find the center of the pom-pom. Apply a generous amount of hot glue to the center. This is where half of the legs will be adhered, so make sure there is enough glue to hold all the pipe cleaners.

6 Stick half of the legs into the hot glue. Stick half of your legs all together into the hot glue. Hold the pom-pom around the pipe cleaners while the glue is setting to secure the legs in place. Repeat on the other side of the pom-pom with the remaining legs.

7 Adjust the legs. To make joints in the legs, bend the pipe cleaners. Try to bend them in roughly the same spot so the legs are fairly uniform and so the spider sits evenly on its feet.

8 Add eyes. Use googly eyes, buttons, beads, pieces of felt, or mini pom-poms for the spider's eyes. Apply the eyes to the pom-pom with hot glue, taking extra care not to burn yourself if the eyes are small. Hold the eyes in place until the glue has set. Extra embellishments could also be added, like a hair bow, a bowtie, a crown, or even a necklace!

thankful

FAUX-EMBROIDERED SWEATSHIRT

materials + tools

- Yarn
  - Medium-weight acrylic, braided medium-weight acrylic, or medium to bulky polyester
  - 1 color
  - About 3 yards (2.7 m)
- Pencil
- Tracing paper
- Scissors
- Sweatshirt
- Fabric glue
- "Thankful" template on page 164

I have tried my hand at many different fiber arts (some more successfully than others!). I have crocheted, knitted, cross-stitched, weaved, sewed, felted, punch-needled, and more. One thing that I have yet to do is embroidery. I know it is similar to cross-stitch, but something about it intimidates me! I will give it a try one of these days, but, in the meantime, I created a project that looks like embroidery but uses glue instead of stitching. It was important to me in this project that the yarn wouldn't peel off or fray in the wash. I tried several brands of fabric glue and about ten types of yarn to find the best combination. There was one clear winner for the glue: Aleene's Fabric Fusion. Other fabric glues may work for you, but this was the best of the ones I tried. The yarn winners are listed in the materials list below. I still recommend washing this sweatshirt inside out and hanging to dry, just to treat the faux embroidery as gently as possible!

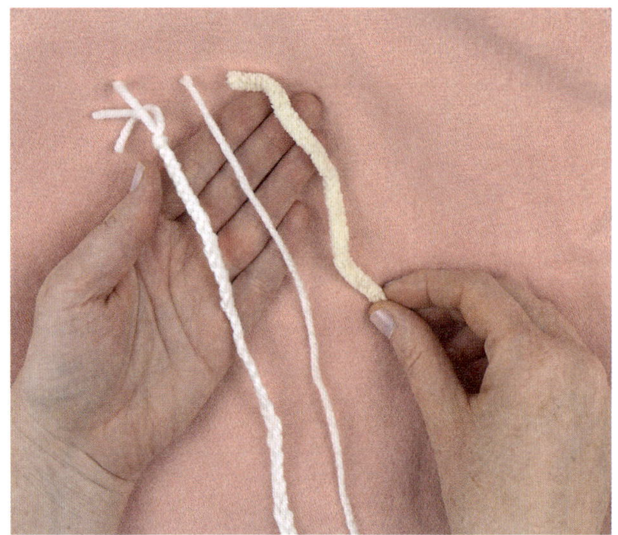

1 Select the yarn. Three types of yarn held up best in the wash during my testing. Bulky polyester yarn (right) did well; three strands of medium weight acrylic yarn braided together (left) also did well. The yarn I used for this tutorial is regular medium acrylic yarn (middle). It is thin enough for details but also doesn't fray as easily.

2 Prepare the template and tracing paper. Photocopy the template on page 164. This template is already a mirror image because it will be traced onto tracing paper, then transferred to the sweatshirt. Lay a piece of tracing paper on top of the template.

3 Trace the template. With a pencil, trace the backward "thankful" onto the tracing paper. Try to make the marks fairly dark. It may help to go over the pencil lines twice. Darker lines will be easier to see when making the transfer.

4 Lay the tracing paper onto the sweatshirt. Flip the tracing paper over so that it is now displaying correctly. Center the paper onto the front of the sweatshirt. Try not to rub the paper onto the sweatshirt while positioning it, since this could transfer the pencil accidentally.

5 Rub the transfer onto the sweatshirt. Using a pencil, ruler, or other flat-edged item, rub the tracing paper to transfer the pencil marks to the sweatshirt. Hold the paper in place so that it doesn't move during the transfer.

6 Glue the yarn to the sweatshirt. Carefully apply fabric glue to the pencil marks for just the first few letters. Make the line of glue about the same width as your yarn. Don't use too much glue, though, or it may show up when dry. Pay extra attention to the yarn ends so that they are securely glued down.

7 Glue in sections. Working in sections, stick the yarn to the glue. Work a few letters at a time so that the glue doesn't dry as you're working. If there is a break in the letters, cut the yarn and begin the new letter. Allow the glue to dry for about two hours, then cover the entire design with something heavy, like a book, and let dry overnight.

tip

Prewash your sweatshirt to make sure the colors don't run.

CANDY CANES

materials + tools

- Yarn
  - Medium-weight acrylic or cotton
  - 2–3 colors
  - About 8 yards (7.3 m) total per candy cane
- **8 mm cotton cord or rope**
- **12-gauge wire or thinner wire doubled up**
- **Wire cutters (optional)**
- **Scissors**
- **Tape**
- **Yarn needle**

Several years ago, wrapped-rope rainbows became a popular craft. Rope was wrapped with yarn, then pieces were stitched together into a rainbow shape. I made many of these colorful decorations, and, while creating a rainbow one day, I accidentally made one of the arcs look a little like a candy cane. That accident led me to one of my favorite Christmas crafts: wrapped-rope candy canes! The trick with these candy canes is to add a piece of wire in with the rope to help the candy cane hold its shape. Unlike the rainbows, which hold their arc shape by being stitched and pulled together, these candy canes must hold their shape on their own. Once you get this technique down, you will want to make a whole tree full of these delicious decorations!

1 Cut the rope and separate the strands. Cut two or three pieces of rope into 10"–12" (25–31 cm) lengths. Separate the strands of each length of rope. Rope usually has about three distinct strands, and separating the rope will give the candy cane fluffier ends and a fuller, more uniform shape.

2 Cut the wire. The wire should be 1"–2" (2.5–5 cm) shorter than the rope so that it isn't poking out at the ends. Use scissors or wire cutters to cut it, depending on the thickness of the wire. If the wire is thinner, cut two or three pieces of wire instead of just one.

3 Enclose the wire inside the rope strands. Put the wire in the center of the rope strands, doing your best to surround the wire with the strands. The wire should be hidden as much as possible inside the rope.

4 Tape the wire and rope. Wrap clear tape around the wire-and-rope bundle in three spots. This will make it easier to wrap with yarn in the coming steps. Check to make sure the rope is still hidden inside the bundle.

5 **Tie yarn onto the rope.** Double-knot your chosen base color of yarn at the bottom of the rope. Leave about 1" (2.5 cm) or so of rope fringe below the knot. The yarn end will get covered in the next step, so don't trim it.

6 **Wrap the yarn around the rope.** Begin wrapping the yarn around the rope, doing your best to wrap as tightly as possible, since this will help make the candy cane more bendable at the end. Wrap over the yarn tail and pieces of tape while making sure that the rope isn't visible under the yarn.

7 **Wrap to the end.** Keep wrapping until there is about 1" (2.5 cm) of rope fringe at the end, just like at the other end. Cut the yarn, leaving a long end. This long end will help secure the yarn later and will be easier to thread into a yarn needle.

8 **Knot the yarn.** Make a loop with the yarn, feed the end through the loop, and pull to tighten. Add a double knot if desired, but it isn't strictly necessary, since the end will be secured more tightly in the next step.

9 **Secure the yarn end.** Thread the yarn needle with the yarn end. Insert the needle under several strands of yarn and pull through. This will secure and hide your end. If you're working with children, you can use a dab of hot glue instead of a needle.

10 **Trim the yarn end.** Cut the remaining tail of the yarn so that it is as close to the candy cane as possible. This gives the candy cane a more polished look, with fewer loose ends.

11 **Attach the yarn for the stripes.** Like in step 5, tie a different color of yarn onto the rope, leaving a long end. Make a double knot with the yarn. This end will also be stitched in, since it cannot be covered by wrapping the yarn.

12 **Secure the yarn end.** Just like in step 9, thread the yarn needle with the end of the second color and insert it under several strands of yarn. Pull the yarn through. Trim the end as close to the candy cane as possible.

13 **Wind the yarn in a stripe design.** Wrap the yarn in a stripe design to the other end. Like in step 8, make a loop, feed the end through the loop, and tighten. Double-knot if desired, but this end will also be secured with a needle.

14 **Secure the yarn end.** Like in steps 9 and 12, thread the yarn end through the yarn needle and pull through several strands of yarn. Trim as close to the candy cane as possible. Repeat steps 11–14 if you want to add a second stripe color.

15 **Trim the rope ends.** Make the rope ends even and neat by trimming each side. Make sure to leave some fringe, since that helps give the candy cane its charm. If any wire is poking out from the rope ends, trim that down as well.

16 **Bend into candy-cane shape.** Give the candy cane its signature look by bending it into shape. This same technique can be used to make other shapes as well. Two candy canes can even be attached to make a cute heart!

GIANT ORNAMENTS

materials + tools

- Yarn
  - Any weight and texture
  - At least 5–6 different colors/weights/textures to give the pom-pom a scrappy look
  - About 20–50 yards (18.3–45.7 m) of yarn*
- **Bowl with a 5"–6" (12.5–15 cm) diameter**
- **Cardboard**
- **Pen or pencil**
- **Scraps of ribbon, fabric, tulle, tinsel, etc.**
- **Embroidery scissors**
- **Trimming scissors**

*Yarn amounts will vary depending on the weight of yarn and size of pom-pom maker.

One of my all-time favorite craft-supply purchases is a really large pom-pom maker. This pom-pom maker can make pom-poms that are 5"–6" (12.5–15 cm) in diameter. They are BIG! I wanted to buy another to send to a friend, but, after searching high and low, I couldn't find another like it. Luckily, I found that it can be easily replicated with a cereal bowl and cardboard. The cardboard maker works just as well, and actually, I now use the cardboard maker more often than the plastic one! I fell in love with making these big pom-poms and have made some for almost every holiday. I hung these giant pom-poms on my Christmas tree, and they added the perfect amount of cheer and coziness. The large size makes these perfect for including scraps of ribbon, fabric, tulle, and tinsel in with the yarn. I often call these "scrappy giant pom-poms" for that reason.

1 Trace the bowl. Grab a box from the recycling bin. A heavier cardboard like a shipping box works best and doesn't bend as easily. Collect two similar pieces and trace around the cereal bowl on both pieces.

2 Cut into a "C" shape. Make a large cardboard pom-pom maker by cutting the traced circles into "Cs." This is just like a small cardboard pom-pom maker from the pom-pom instructions on page 24—but larger!

3 Wrap the yarn. Just like in the basic instructions on page 24, wrap the yarn around both pieces of cardboard. Use yarn of many textures and weights and add pieces of ribbon, tinsel, fabric, etc. as desired.

4 Wrap until the center is full. To get the fullest pom-pom, wind yarn around the maker until there is no space left in the center. Only the two cardboard ends of the pom-pom maker will still be uncovered.

5 **Cut through the yarn.** Insert sharp scissors in between the circles of cardboard and cut through the yarn. It's important to make sure to hold the bottom of the pom-pom maker and the yarn tightly with your other hand while cutting so that it doesn't all fall apart.

6 **Tie the pom-pom.** While still holding the maker with one hand, slide another piece of yarn in between the circles of cardboard. Gather all the yarn pieces in the maker and knot tightly. To get it extra tight, wrap the yarn piece around the maker twice before knotting. Remove the pom-pom from the cardboard.

7 **Trim the pom-pom.** Start giving your pom-pom its haircut. Part of the charm of this pom-pom comes from its "scrappy" look, so don't trim it too perfectly. The long ends from the piece used for tying the pom-pom can be used to hang it, so leave these long.

8 **Finish the pom-pom.** Trim around the pom-pom to even it out, making sure not to accidentally cut the long ends for hanging. Your ornament is ready to display! Repeat the steps to create as many as you'd like.

materials + tools

- Yarn
  - Super-fine, fine, light, medium, or bulky-weight acrylic, cotton, or Omegacryl
  - 2–3 shades of green
  - For a 3" (7.5 cm) long tassel: about 6 yards (5.5 m) per tassel*
- Tassel maker
- Scissors
- Yarn needle
- Mini pom-poms
- Hot-glue gun

*Yarn amounts will vary depending on the weight of yarn and length of tassel.

TASSEL-TREE ORNAMENTS

The shape of a tassel lends itself perfectly to a cute Christmas tree. By stacking three (or more!) tassels, you can create a fuller tassel and a perfectly tiered, festive tree. I like combining different shades of green to add extra color and dimension. This can be a fun craft with kids, since the tassels can be made in advance, then kids can choose their colors and help decorate their trees with embellishments. I have used this same technique to make colorful, tiered tassels for door hangers, bag key chains, and bookmarks. Instead of using just green yarn, use a variety of colors to make a darling tassel key chain to hang from your bag or door!

1 **Make three tassels.** Using a tassel maker or a piece of cardboard, make three small tassels in three different shades of green that are each about the same length and thickness. Refer to the basic tassel instructions on page 20 if needed.

2 **String the yarn needle.** Thread the needle with a long piece of yarn. It is better to cut the piece too long rather than too short—any extra can be trimmed at the end. Once the needle is threaded, double up the yarn by tying a knot at the bottom.

3 **Insert the needle into the bottom tassel.** Choose which tassel will be the bottom of the tree. Flip the tassel over and move the fringe aside to find the center. Insert the needle into the center and pull the needle up through the center of the top of the tassel.

4 **Pull the yarn into the tassel.** Don't pull the yarn all the way through the tassel—pull only until the knot touches the center of the tassel. If you pull too hard, the yarn might go all the way through.

5 **String the remaining tassels.** Repeat steps 3 and 4 for the other two tassels. Just like with the first tassel, don't pull too hard—just pull the needle through and push the tassel until the center is touching the top of the one below it.

6 **Push the tassels close together.** Make sure the tassels are not smashing each other, or they will become misshapen. Each one should be lightly touching the one above and below it. Fluff the fringe of the top two tassels to evenly cover the tassels below them.

7 **Knot the yarn string.** Cut the yarn so that the needle can be removed from it. Take these two ends of yarn and make a knot to create a loop for hanging. The yarn can be trimmed down if the loop is going to be bigger than you want it to be.

8 **Glue mini pom-poms to the tassels.** If desired, hot-glue mini pom-poms as ornaments on your tree. Other embellishments could include small bows, sequins, paper stars, or mini ornaments. Children could use school glue instead of hot glue.

MINI SNOW HATS

Why are mini-sized things always so cute? I received a dollhouse for Christmas when I was eight, and I think that is when my love of miniature items started. I used to make tiny books out of paper and tiny foods out of clay for my dollhouse. I would wander the miniatures aisle at the craft store, buying tiny pots and pans and mini pretend art supplies. Everything is just darling in miniature! I just love this mini snow-hat craft because the hats are irresistibly cute and small. They also look like they should be difficult to craft, but they are actually very simple! Make a bunch and hang them from your tree or string them onto a garland for a sweet, wintery vibe.

materials + tools

- **Yarn**
  - Medium, bulky, or super-bulky weight
  - 1 color
  - About 20–40 12" (31 cm) pieces (will depend on yarn thickness)
- **Toilet paper roll**
- **Scissors**
- **Cotton ball**
- **Yarn needle**
- **Mini pom-poms or embellishments (optional)**
- **School glue (optional)**

1 **Cut the toilet-paper tube.** Cut a small section from the toilet-paper tube that measures about ½"–¾" (1.5–2 cm) in height. This will be the band of the hat, so cutting the section too small or too large could make the finished hat look misshapen.

2 **Make a yarn loop.** Cut 20–40 pieces of yarn into 12" (31 cm) lengths. The number will vary depending on the thickness of the yarn. Take one of the pieces of yarn, fold it in half, and lay a loop on the outside of the tube.

3 **Pull the ends through the loop.** Wrap the ends of the yarn through the inside of the tube, then pull the ends through the loop. All the strands will be tied in this same way, working from the outside to the inside.

4 **Tighten the knot.** Make a knot by pulling the ends down on the outside of the tube. Tighten to make sure the yarn stays in place. The knot should be at the bottom of the tube.

5 **Repeat all the way around.** Repeat this process until the entire tube is covered with yarn. Make sure to always tie the yarn in the same direction so that it looks uniform. All the knots should be at the bottom.

6 **Push the yarn ends through the tube.** Push the yarn ends up through the inside of the tube, leaving the knots at the bottom. The tube will become the rim of the hat. It will resemble a jellyfish when all yarn is pushed through.

tip

To turn these hats into a garland, use a needle to string through the hat right below each top pom-pom.

7 Tie the hat together. Using another piece of yarn, tie a knot around the fringe. The knot should be about halfway or three-quarters of the way toward the ends of the yarn. Trim the fringe to create a small pom-pom shape.

8 Add a yarn hanger. String a piece of yarn onto a yarn needle and double-knot the ends. Insert the needle through the top of the hat and pull carefully until the knot catches underneath the knot you tied in step 7. Don't pull too hard or the knot may go through. Cut the yarn to remove the needle, then knot the top strings to secure the hanging loop.

9 Insert a cotton ball. To help the hat hold its shape, insert one or two cotton balls up inside the hat. If desired, add embellishments to the hat using school glue and mini pom-poms, sequins, fake snow, etc.

CREATIVE WRAPPING

materials + tools

- Yarn
  - Various textures and weights
  - Various colors
  - As much as you need!
- **Wrapping paper (simple patterned or plain paper works well)**
- **Tape**
- **Pencil**
- **Hot-glue gun**
- **Pom-pom maker**
- **Scissors**
- **Embroidery scissors**
- **Gift toppers like mini snow hats (page 144), candy canes (page 130), giant pom-poms (page 136), or tree tassels (page 140)**
- **Embellishments**

I am a big believer in making gifts look cute! I think that presentation is half the gift. A really simple gift can be elevated with a little extra thought when wrapping. The wrapping materials don't need to be expensive, either. In fact, most of the time, a simple wrapping paper with yarn scraps is all you need to take wrapping to the next level. I also love using items I've made as part of the gift. At Christmas, I use items like the mini snow hats, giant pom-poms, and candy canes as gift toppers. These make the gifts look darling, and the recipients get an extra gift to keep!

Tie bows on a box. Wrap a gift using a plain or simply patterned paper. Using various types of yarn, tie bows all over the gift. Stagger the bows so that they don't line up right on top of each other. This wrapping method works best for boxed gifts.

Add a name with yarn. Wrap a gift in plain paper. Trace a name on the top of the gift with a pencil. Hot-glue yarn to the tracing to embellish the name. Medium to bulky yarn works well. This wrapping method works best for boxed gifts.

Add a giant pom-pom topper. Use a giant pom-pom (page 136) to add a very fluffy topper to a gift. When making the pom-pom, leave the tying string long so that it can be easily attached to the gift and then used as a decoration after.

Make a scrappy bow. Wrap one piece of yarn around the gift, knotting it once. Add pieces of yarn, ribbon, tinsel, etc. on top of the knot, then knot again with the same piece of yarn. This gives the scraps a bow-like look.

Add a gift topper. Wrap a piece of yarn around the gift, knotting it once. Add gift toppers on top of the knot, then use the yarn to knot again, securing the gift toppers. Additional treats like candies, bottle-brush trees, or tiny toys could also be added to the top.

Make a yarn Christmas tree. Tape a long piece of green yarn to the back of a gift. Wrap the yarn around and around the package in a triangular shape. Move the strands around if needed to get the tree shape. Tape the final yarn end to the back.

Add embellishments to the tree. Tiny pom-poms can be used as ornaments, and a big pom-pom can be the tree topper. You could also tie real mini ornaments to the yarn tree for the recipient to keep after unwrapping the gift!

FINGER-LOOP WREATH

materials + tools

- Yarn
  - Bulky finger-loop yarn in acrylic or polyester
  - 1 color
  - For a 15" (38 cm) wreath form: about 30 yards (27.4 m)
- Wreath form, either straw or foam
- Hot-glue gun
- Scissors
- Yarn, ribbon, or fabric (or a combination of these) for embellishments

Projects that look like they must have been difficult to make but that are actually very simple are some of the best. A finger-loop yarn wreath is one of those projects! The texture of this wreath makes it look as though it would be complicated and time consuming, but it couldn't be easier. The key is the finger-loop yarn, which is often used for making blankets. Instead of using the yarn to finger-weave, the yarn is simply hot-glued to a wreath form. When the loops are glued upright to the form, they create a soft and cozy wreath that's perfect for any season. The finished product looks like something you could buy at a high-end boutique. For even more cuteness, ribbons and bows can be layered and attached to the top. I have made several of these wreaths over the years as gifts, and they are always a hit!

1 Hot-glue the yarn to the wreath form. Put a line of hot glue onto the wreath form. If you're using a straw form, keep the plastic wrap around the wreath if possible; it keeps the straw from making a mess. Lay the end of the yarn onto the glue, with the loops facing up.

2 Wrap the yarn around the form. Keep the loops facing upward and outward, laying only the base of the yarn onto the wreath form. With every few wraps around, apply another line of glue to help hold the yarn in place.

3 Continue wrapping and gluing. While wrapping, push the yarn close together so that none of the wreath form is showing. Make sure the loops are always facing out. When one skein runs out, glue the end to the wreath and start another skein by gluing the beginning of the new skein right where the old skein ends.

4 Finish the wreath. Keep wrapping the yarn all the way around the form. Hot-glue the yarn in the final remaining empty space. There may be more space on the outside of the form than on the inside. Fluff up the yarn on the outside to cover any extra gaps if necessary.

5 Tie a hanger onto the wreath. Using a piece of yarn or ribbon, add a hanger to the wreath. Feed the yarn through the center, then tie it at the top. This wreath will be a little heavier if you're using a straw form, so use a strong yarn or ribbon.

6 **Add yarn and ribbon embellishments.** Decide how long to make your yarn fringe, then double that length, since the yarn will be doubled up. Cut the desired strands. Slide the center of all the strands under the yarn used for hanging the wreath.

7 **Tie the embellishments to the wreath.** Use a thinner string or piece of yarn, gather up the pieces of yarn and ribbon, and tie them to the hanging string. All pieces should now be tied together. The hanging string can be pulled up or down so that the fringe falls to the desired height.

SNOW GARLAND

materials + tools

- Yarn
  - Medium to bulky-weight acrylic or cotton
  - White and cream in various shades/weights/textures
  - For a 48" (122 cm) garland: about 70 yards (64 m)
- **White cotton crochet thread**
- **Scissors**
- **Metal needle with an eye large enough for the thread to fit**

I'm personally more of a sunshine fan than a snow fan, but since I've lived for a long time now in a state with snow, I have learned to see the beauty in it. Everything looks lovely when it's covered in fresh, sparkling snow. I still do everything I can to avoid having to drive in it, but I do appreciate sitting in a cozy house and watching the snow falling. This snow garland plays off those fluffy snowflakes, but instead of having to go out in the cold to see them, this garland can be enjoyed in the comfort of your warm house. While this garland is made with white and cream yarn, various colors could easily be swapped in to make different variations. Bright colors could be fun for a party or holiday. Put on a good show or audiobook, sit by the fire, and get stringing!

1 **Cut the crochet thread.** Drape a long strand of crochet thread in the location and manner in which you want to use your finished garland (e.g., with many long drapes, or a few shallow drapes). Then cut the thread a little longer than your planned garland, since it is easier to start with too much than to end with too little!

2 **Cut pieces of white yarn.** Cut small pieces of various shades and weights of white and cream yarn. Make the pieces about 1 ½"–2 ½" (4–6.5 cm) in length. This project requires a lot of yarn pieces, so get comfy cutting! More can always be cut later if needed.

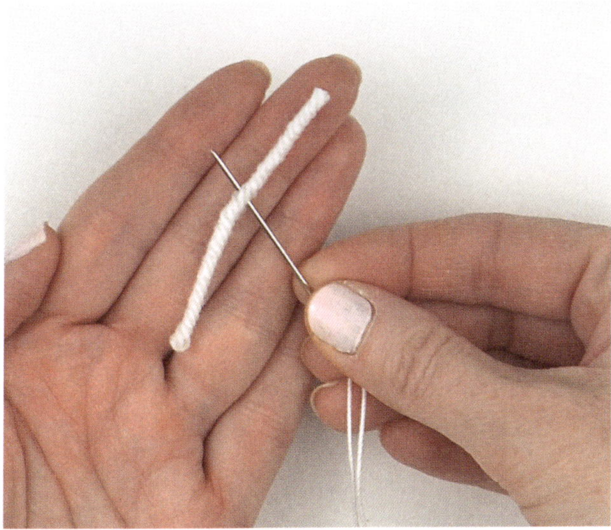

3 **String the needle through the pieces of yarn.** Thread the needle with the long piece of crochet thread. No knots are necessary right now. String the needle through the center of a single piece of yarn. The yarn is thin, so make sure the needle goes into the center—and take care not to get poked.

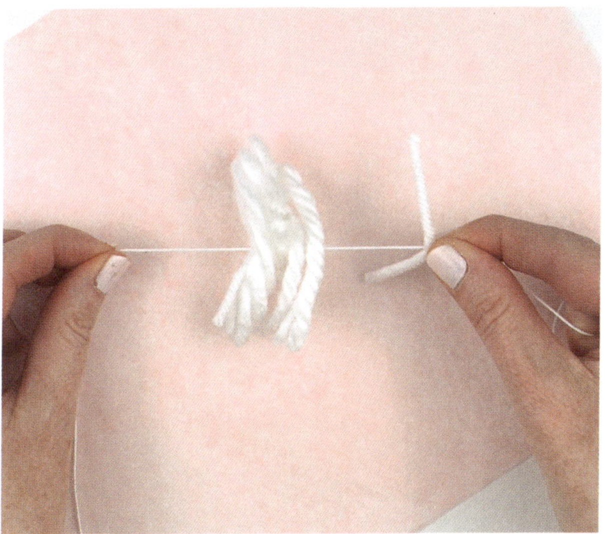

4 **Continue stringing the yarn to the end.** Continue to add piece after piece of yarn in this same way. Push the pieces of yarn close together as you go. They will naturally sit in different directions, which gives the garland its fluffy look. Keep adding pieces until you reach your desired length. Add knots at the beginning and end of the string.

3

TEMPLATES

In this final section of the book, you'll find a handful of helpful templates for making a few of the projects. Trace or photocopy these items out of the book as needed. Except for the pegboard and wire-grid templates (which are for visual reference only), the templates are presented at 100% actual size.

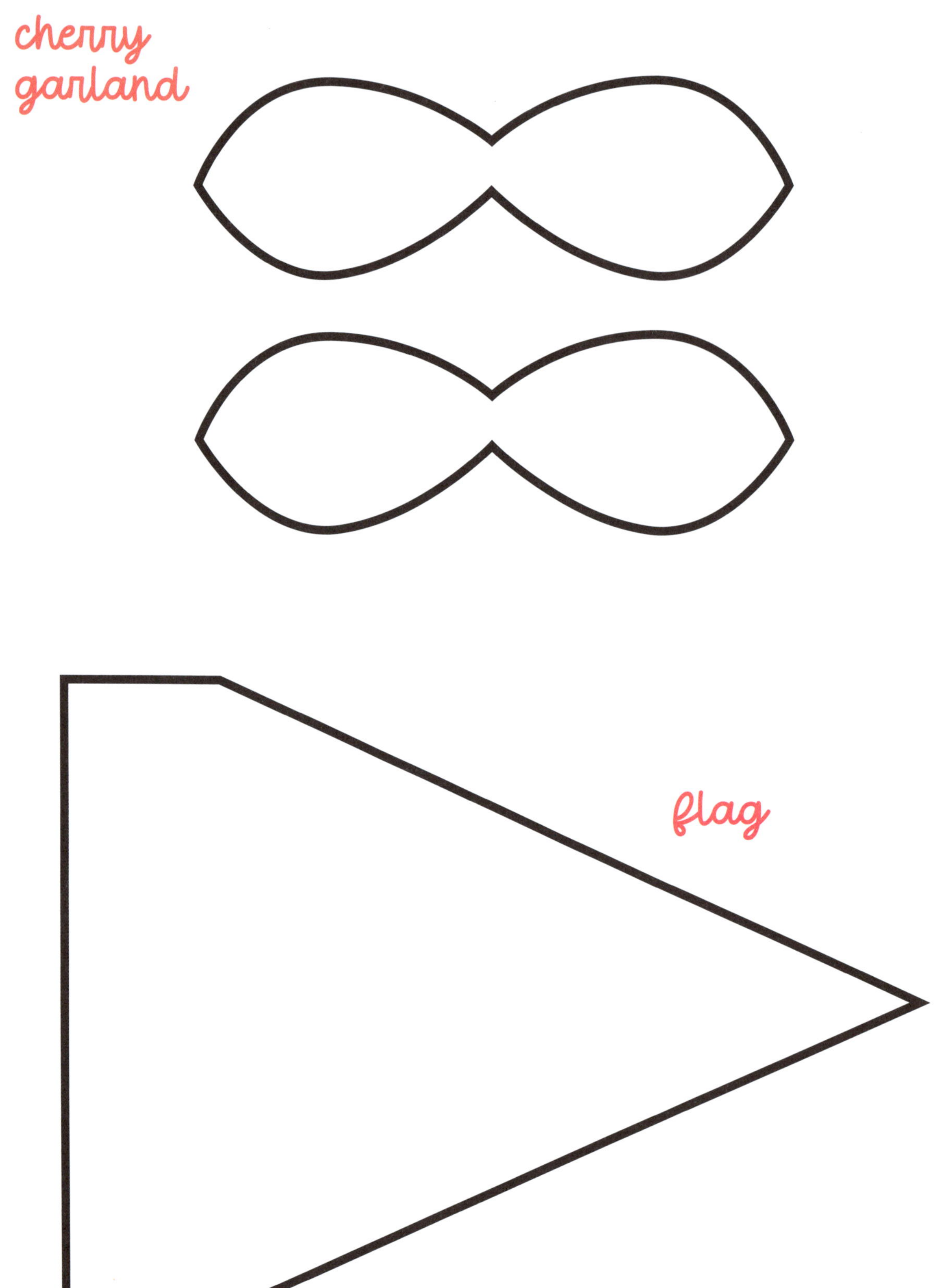
cherry garland
flag

cross-stitch pegboard

faux-embroidered sweatshirt

stitched wire grid

Sarah Freeman is a professional crafter, content creator, and the creative force behind @apricotpolkadot, a colorful blog that helps others find joy through creating and making. An English teacher turned full-time maker, Sarah began her crafting journey in 2015 by selling whimsical pom-pom garlands on Etsy. Since then, she has grown a loyal following through her blog, YouTube tutorials, and Instagram, inspiring others with approachable, joy-filled fiber projects. Her work has been featured in *Mollie Makes*, *HGTV Magazine*, and over 25 segments on Utah's popular lifestyle show *Studio 5*. Sarah resides in South Jordan, Utah, with her husband and four children. You can usually find her with yarn or embroidery floss in her hands, but when she isn't busy crafting or chauffeuring her kids around, she loves reading, vacationing at the beach, cheering on her kids in their various activities, and baking chocolate-chip oatmeal cookies. You can follow along with her crafting adventures at www.apricotpolkadot.com or on Instagram @apricotpolkadot.

INDEX

Note: Page numbers in *italics* indicate projects and templates (in parentheses).

BETTER DAY BOOKS®

HAPPY • CREATIVE • CURATED

Business is personal at Better Day Books. We were founded on the belief that all people are creative and that making things by hand is inherently good for us. It's important to us that you know how much we appreciate your support. The book you are holding in your hands was crafted with the artistic passion of the author and brought to life by a team of wildly enthusiastic creatives who believed it could inspire you. If it did, please drop us a line and let us know about it. Connect with us on Instagram, post a photo of your art, and let us know what other creative pursuits you are interested in learning about. It all matters to us. You're kind of a big deal.

it's a good day to have a better day!®

www.betterdaybooks.com

better_day_books